Preferred Lies About Golf

*The Real Low-down on the
Royal and Ancient Game*

Peter Dobereiner

Illustrated by John Ireland

PERENNIAL LIBRARY

Harper & Row, Publishers, New York
Cambridge, Philadelphia, San Francisco
London, Mexico City, São Paulo, Singapore, Sydney

A hardcover edition of this book was published in Great Britain in 1987 by Stanley Paul & Co. Ltd, an imprint of Century Hutchinson Ltd. It is here reprinted by arrangement with Stanley Paul & Co. Ltd, an imprint of Century Hutchinson Ltd.

First PERENNIAL LIBRARY edition was published in 1989

LIBRARY OF CONGRESS CATALOG CARD NUMBER 88-45553

ISBN 0-06-097209-2

89 90 91 92 93 FG 10 9 8 7 6 5 4 3 2 1

For Craig

Contents

Foreword

Just as ship builders re-enact the *Titanic* disaster with the ritual of a collision between a new vessel and the symbolic iceberg of a champagne bottle, and actors cry 'Break a leg' on opening night, and Portuguese fishermen paint eyes on the prow of their boats to see them safely back to port, so we literati have our little superstition to ward off the evil eye. We launch a book with the sacred incantation: 'All the characters in this book are fictitious. Any similarity to any person, living or dead, is purely coincidental.'

Of course it is sheer mumbo jumbo; no libel lawyer worth his brief would be deterred for a second by such a disclaimer. Even so, it is with the trepidation of a man forced at gunpoint to walk under a ladder that I break the tradition and omit the magic phrase, but there is nothing else for it. In this case it would be quite inappropriate because the characters are patently not fictitious. They are real people represented in fictional terms.

In the case of the worst of the villains I have selected the names of golf-writing colleagues, confident that I have enough dirt on them to keep their lawyers safely holstered. The heroes are golfers who may or may not be flattered by their portraits. George Bernard Shaw justified taking liberties with the literal truth for the sake of a greater veracity and that has been my intention, to turn real people into fictitious characters in fictitious situations in order to illuminate their virtues.

Does that sound grovelling? So it is intended. In the unlikely event that anyone depicted in this book should say to himself: 'Hello, that's a bit strong. This loathsome hack is holding me up to public hatred, ridicule and contempt. Now what was the name of that ambulance-chaser with the close-set eyes who I played with in a pro-am the other day . . .?' I counsel caution.

In defamation cases you only hit the real pay dirt if you can turn up genuine malice. That, in my case, is impossible. You see, I have a defective liver which is incapable of secreting bile, a dreadful handicap for a writer. If I set out to expose, ruthlessly and fearlessly, a mass murderer who beats his wife and nudges his ball in the semi-rough the result comes out as a hagiography, a paeon of gushing praise which makes him sound like a secular saint.

In short, I am subverted by brotherly love for all mankind, golfers included, and pathologically disqualified from intentionally inflicting pain. My only purpose in writing this book was to make the principal characters more famous, better loved and even richer as a consequence.

1

In the Very Beginning

(And Two Hundred Years Previously)

It was the time of the Senzie fair. Market Street was packed along its full length with stalls. The crowds were so dense, jostling and shouting and laughing at the curious cries of the foreign pedlars, that it required a considerable physical effort to move about. The Laird o' Piscottie lowered his head and, using the purposeful technique which had won him the No. 6 jersey in the St Andrews University first XV, bored through the human thicket, side-stepping a dancing bear and scattering an impromptu meeting of the St Andrews lodging-house keepers' association just as those worthies were reaching a consensus to raise their prices by a factor of three for the entire month. Finally the Laird saw his objective, his shepherd boys Angus and Donald crouched by a wicket pen containing his twelve prime sheep. The sheep were coughing pitifully, choking on the acrid smoke blowing up from South Street where the ecclesiastical authorities were burning the latest cull of martyrs. The Laird considered the effect on potential customers of bronchial merchandise. There was no hurry to dispose of the sheep because the market for mutton would stay strong for several days, possibly rising by a groat or two. 'Take them down by the beach onto the linksland where the air is clean and the grass is lush,' he commanded. 'It is common land so we might as well fatten them up for a few days at public expense.'

The boys did as they were bid and, true enough, the air was indeed sweet along the sea front. Of course, this was long before the days of civilized amenities such as the outfall sewer which today pours noxious effluent into the sea just upwind of the Royal and Ancient clubhouse and which makes bathing such an adventure.

The sheep quickly fell to grazing the succulent grasses and Donald, having nothing better to do, took an idle swipe at a pebble with his crook. The pebble scuttled over the turf.

'I've been hitting pebbles for a bit,' said Angus, 'and I've found that if you take your knife and cut a flat side to the handle of the crook, slightly angled with what I call loft, then the pebble flies through the air.'

Donald whittled away at his crook and tried again. This time the pebble rose into the air but curled sharply to the left.

'I had the same trouble,' said Angus. 'Try moving your right hand a wee bitty over the top of the shaft.' Donald did so and his next pebble flew straight and true. 'Fantastic!' he said. 'With this grip I bet I could hit my pebble further than yours.'

'How much do you bet?' asked Angus.

'A bite of my sandwich,' said Donald.

'You're on,' said Angus, as he deftly fashioned a small mound of sand on which to place his pebble. Angus lost three bites in succession, and the prospect of losing his entire lunch stimulated his imagination. 'Look, you are bigger than me and you are going to out-hit me every time and both of us will soon get bored. Why don't we combine long hitting with the subtleties of accuracy, tactical challenge and artistry?'

'Like how?'

'Well, you see yon cart gate, with a rabbit hole on the bank? We will play from here, but you have to get your pebble right inside the rabbit hole. The one who puts his pebble into the hole in the fewest number of strokes is the winner.'

'Done,' said Donald, and hit a screamer which flew the best part of twenty yards. With a deft flick Angus holed out with his eleventh stroke. Donald's ball lay a yard from the rabbit hole in nine. He made a tentative pass at his pebble, and it stopped inches from the hole.

'Ne'ir up, ne'ir in,' said Angus.

Since the outcome of the match was undecided they determined to play to another hole, along the dunes towards the Eden estuary. Donald hit another blue-flamer. 'How do you like dem apples?' he enquired smugly. 'Drive for show but putt for bread,' replied Angus.

'That would have more of a ring to it if you said putt for dough,' observed Donald.

Angus won that hole and Donald suggested that they might as well work their way right out to the end of the promontory, playing a series of

'. . . his next pebble flew straight and true.'

holes for the match. So they played a hole across the linksland, then one very heathery hole, followed by a hole to a rabbit scrape on a high ridge.

By now they were really quite adept at striking their pebbles with both power and accuracy. At this point they spied two pedlars, Dutchmen to judge by their wooden shoes, and obviously just landed at the harbour. They were trudging along the track to St Andrews with bundles of Huguenot lace slung from sticks supported on their broad shoulders.

The shepherds accosted the two strangers. 'Good day to you. My name is Angus and this is my friend Donald.'

The first Dutchman clicked his heels and introduced himself. 'Hurts van Rentl.' The second Dutchman did likewise: 'Paul Strijker.'

'It is a long and dreary walk to St Andrews,' said Angus, 'and we were wondering if it might not enliven your journey if you joined us in a healthful pastime we have just invented and which we call pebble-stick. Permit me to show you how it is played.'

The Dutchmen watched with faces as impassive as Edam cheeses while Angus demonstrated his skills and explained the rudimentary rules. 'Would you like to practise a shot or two before we play?'

'No, I don't think so,' said van Rentl, 'it seems perfectly simple.'

Angus winked surreptitiously at Donald. 'We have found that the game is more exciting if we have a small interest on the match, a modest wager.'

'Of course,' said van Rentl, 'I can see how that would make the game more interesting.' He laid down his bundle and withdrew the stout hazel stick which, as Angus now observed, was tipped with a stubby metal head. 'How many sheep do you have in your flock, lad?' he enquired.

'Twelve,' said Donald.

'Very well,' said van Rentl. 'We'll play a four-sheep Nassau, covered by the equivalent value in fine lace, with automatic presses, oozalums, greenies and golden ferrets, four ball better ball, or better pebble in your case. You're up.'

Although thoroughly bemused by this recital Donald managed to clip his pebble a creditable distance, the best part of fifteen yards. Angus also hit a good one.

Paul Strijker now drew from his pouch a small white ball of stitched leather which he placed carefully on a tuffet. He took two practice swings, stepped up to his ball and made a languid pass at it with his hazel stick. The ball completely vanished, or so it seemed to Angus and Donald. But

4

the Dutchman, balanced on one leg like a heron, was staring intently up into the sky and muttering to himself: 'Blow, wind, blow. That's good. Get in the hole, my beauty!'

The shepherds followed his gaze and spied the ball, a diminishing white dot against the blue sky. It seemed to hang in the air and then fall, landing about ten yards from the rabbit hole and bouncing to a halt. Van Rentl, saying something about giving her a bit of a sliding fade, hit an almost identical shot.

As they hacked their pebbles forlornly towards the target, both requiring fifteen strokes, the shepherds paced off the distance to the hole. It came to 275 yards.

The rest of the story is too painful to relate in detail, but you can guess the general drift.

'We goofed,' said Angus.

'Aye, we're a pair of goofers,' said Donald.

While Strijker idly sketched a design for a lace mat for the tourist market with a representation of the cathedral and the legend 'St Andrews, home of goof', van Rentl said: 'Look, we can't leave you completely destitute. Take our sticks, or kolbes as we call them, and a supply of our balls. We've plenty more at home. Practise hard and when you can hit 250 out of a cuppy lie and hold the ball up in a forty-mile-per-hour crosswind that will be time enough to look out for pigeons.'

With that the Dutchmen were gone, driving the sheep towards the market.

'I bet there are plenty of pigeons across the water there at Carnoustie,' said Donald.

'Are there any Dutchmen at Carnoustie?' asked Angus.

'Not that I know of,' said Donald.

'Then that's where we'll go,' said Angus.

So the game of goof put down its tentative roots into the fertile soil of Scotland.

2
Scotland's Plan for Salvation

Golf historians have commented on the keen interest taken in golf by all the kings of the House of Stuart, although no scholar has explained why this should be. After all, there were many diversions of a far more exciting nature available to Scottish monarchs in the Middle Ages. Quite apart from the regular fixture list of wars with the English, the Scottish kings had ample opportunities for friendlies against rebellious factions within Scotland. Massacring Campbells, for instance, was esteemed to be capital sport and between whiles there was always scope for barbecuing Papists or Protestants according to the season. Golf must have been tedious in comparison with plotting the assassination of recalcitrant lairds, and yet the Stuart kings were all obsessed by golf. How come? In order to solve this mystery we must consider the nature of Scotland itself. The country was desperately poor, ill-favoured by nature with an inhospitable climate and no mineral wealth, just mile after mile of bogs and granite mountain ranges.

The second King James, known as James II, was ambitious for his country and pondered deeply on how to make Scotland's fortune. There was, after all, limited scope in stealing English cattle across the border.

In those days kings, like golf clubs, were known by their whimsical nicknames rather than by number and James the Flying Right Elbow reasoned that the best way to grow rich, indeed the only way, would be to lure wealthy visitors to Scotland and then rob them. These days tourist boards all over the world work on this principle, but in the fifteenth century it was a radical idea and James had to pioneer the fine detail. He ordered parchment and pen to be delivered to his chamber, along with a stoup of ale, and settled down to a long planning session. At the top of one sheet of parchment he wrote:

Question: How on earth could any rational (and wealthy) foreigner be persuaded to visit Scotland?

On the second sheet he wrote:

Question: Assuming that we can attract them, how can we prevent the mugs from catching the next boat home without even unpacking?

He became so absorbed in his task that his stoup of ale sat neglected by the hearth. In time the brew began to bubble and the chamber filled with steam which, on striking the chill of the royal crown, condensed into droplets. These in due course formed into rivulets which flowed down his face and saturated his moustache. A heady odour attracted the King's attention. He passed the tip of his tongue along his moustache and the moisture produced a pleasing tingle. Being a man of scientific bent the King analysed the nature of this phenomenon and in quick order he hung his full suit of armour near the window and placed his chamber pot beneath it to catch the condensed droplets as they coursed down the metal. Soon there was enough liquid for him to fill his goblet which he drained at one draught. 'Wow!' he croaked, catching his breath, 'but this crown water packs quite a wallop.'

He called his Chamberlain and bid him try the liquor. 'Faith, siree,' said the Chamberlain, 'but it is like drinking fire, albeit beguiling withal.'

They both had another goblet of crown water. 'Methinks it has great potential,' said the King. 'No question,' replied the Chamberlain, 'although we will have to do something about the name.'

A curious euphoria seized the two men. The King threw an arm around the Chamberlain's shoulder. 'You're nae a gad old boat. Shorry, I mean bad old goat, Hamish.'

'See you, Jimmy,' replied the Chamberlain, 'but the name's Rabbie.'

'Shame difference, gad old boat,' said the King, slithering to the floor as the room began to revolve alarmingly. Just before he slipped into oblivion he had a moment of lucidity. At least he had solved the problem of how to keep visitors in Scotland – under the benign sedation of crown water.

The next day the King rose rather later than usual and returned to his task. After working all afternoon he had covered his first parchment with a list of all the tourist attractions that Scotland had to offer. Haggis, bagpipe music, baps, Arbroath smokies, thistles, black pudding, porridge, woolly bonnets, stags at bay, sword dancing, mutton pies, tossing the caber, pawky jokes and puking in the street.

Towards nightfall the King's vision cleared and his head stopped throbbing. One by one he crossed out every item on his list. He was deeply depressed when the Chamberlain entered for his daily audience. 'Don't tell me the English have invaded us again,' he groaned.

'Fear not, sire. What do you want first, the good news or the bad news?'

'Hit me with something to revive my spirits, Hamish!'

'Rabbie, sire.'

'Right! Rabbie.'

'Well, we've come up with a knockout name for the hooch: water of life.'

'Not very catchy,' objected the King.

'It sounds better in Gaelic, sire.'

'Try me,' said the King.

The Chamberlain made a noise like a man trying to dislodge a fish bone from his throat.

'Frankly, Rabbie, I don't see American tourists coping with that.'

'Exactly, sire. That is why we have anglicized it to whisky. By the way I've brought you a bottle from the pilot distillery.'

'And the bad news?'

'The peasants are neglecting their military training because they spend all their spare time kicking a pig's bladder about and sporting at the goof.'

'Goof?'

'Yes, sire, it has taken a terrific hold on popular fancy. It's like a drug.'

Golf: that was the very thing the King had been seeking, something addictive and available only in Scotland. That would pull the tourists, and keep them coming back for more. But it wouldn't do to make a public fuss about it or the English would be sure to steal golf like they did everything else. They would smother England with golf courses and reap all the profits.

'Issue an edict banning this football,' commanded the King. 'Say nothing about golf. In fact, you might privily encourage landowners, the church and the burghs to endow any spare land in perpetuity for the citizens to dig for shells, trap rabbits and desport themselves at the golf.'

The King's grandson, James the Illiterate, in due course issued a similar decree, commanding that 'ye futeball and ye gowfe and ither sich unprofitable sportis be utterlie cryit doune and nicht be usit in all ye realme'. Scholars have assumed that this was another ban, but to anyone with a thorough grounding in mediaeval Scottish dialects the meaning is quite different. To cry down meant to dismiss something as being of no significance and the edict was clearly intended for the English spies, evidence that Scotland had nothing worth pillaging in the sporting line.

Successive Stuart monarchs, James the Incontinent and James of the Rusty Hand-me-down Armour, all pursued their ancestor's dream with zeal. The message rang down the ages: golf is the most fun you can have without taking off your doublet and the only true golf is to be found in Scotland.

By the time the nations were united the association between golf and Scotland was indelibly fixed throughout the kingdom. Every burgh and hamlet in Scotland had workshops and trained artisans at the ready. It was time for the big kill; Scotland was poised to enter the export market with golf equipment, golf teachers and course designers.

The Hundred Years' War and sundry other complications had delayed the big push, but the opportunity came with the era of imperial expansion. The plan had to be executed with subterfuge because the English regarded foreign conquest as a sacred duty, to convert the heathen to Christianity and cricket. 'That is all very well, Mr Disraeli,' observed Queen Victoria, 'but what does England get out of it?'

'We keep what sticks to the shovel, ma'am,' replied the Prime Minister, conjuring up a vision of British ships laden with gold, jute, silk, silver, cotton, rubber, timber, coal, iron ore, maize, beef and mutton, gem stones and guano, whatever that might be.

Scotland's mighty contingent of golf professionals was hurriedly and secretly indoctrinated into the rudiments of military life or civil engineering and insinuated into the expeditionary forces, each man taking with him a supply of clubs and balls.

When these tactics were tried in the New World, with Scottish officers ostentatiously playing golf during lulls in the American War of Independence, the marketing strategy had been all wrong. The former colonials could hardly be expected to take to a game played by men who had been sent to suppress them.

It was all very different in India, Africa, Australia, the Far East and South

'. . . with Scottish officers ostentatiously playing golf during lulls in the American War of Independence.'

America. The ignorant, heathen natives watched the Scots at their pastime and remarked in different tongues but with one voice: 'That looks incredibly easy. Even an ignorant, heathen native like myself could whack a little white ball and it might ingratiate me with these curious people who are so free with their trade goods. Anything's better than that bloody cricket. I think I'll give this golf a try.'

Orders for clubs and balls poured into Scotland. The faith of those Stuart kings had been justified at last. The world readily accepted that a club would not work unless it was stamped with the magic incantation: 'Hand forged in Scotland'.

Alas, having created the demand and opened up the market with such patience and commercial cunning, the Scots ultimately blew it. It was that emphasis on hand craftsmanship that scuppered the great golf conspiracy. The Americans invented mass production and inherited the golfing earth. But at least, having made their fortunes, they descended on Scotland in droves to see where it all began. And that, if you remember, was all a part of the vision of James of the Flying Right Elbow.

3
The Monstrous Regiment of Women

In an act of prophetic justice, Mary Queen of Scots neatly sliced off the top of her breakfast egg. At the far end of the table her consort was absent-mindedly picking at his snack of rashers, fried bread, four eggs, black pudding, fried breakfast cake, tomatoes and chips. Between mouthfuls and quaffs of ale he scratched industriously at a parchment, absorbed in his writing. Eventually he laid aside his quill with a smile of satisfaction.

'Where's your pal?'

'If you are referring to the Earl of Bothwell, I daresay he is sleeping late. He had a hard day yesterday.'

'And a hard night, I shouldn't wonder. I don't trust that smarmy creep.'

'Why ever not?'

'Too good at dancing and a bit too fond of all that hand-kissing stuff. Wouldn't surprise me a bit if one of our wenches finds herself in an interesting condition after he leaves. And I don't like the way he looks at you.'

'Don't be ridiculous, Henry. Lord Bothwell is a cultured man. And that makes a change round here.'

'If you say so. What's your programme for today, another heavy stint ordering the affairs of state?'

'Well, it is such a lovely morning that I thought I would get in a round of goff. The bower of Longniddry has made me up a darling baffie, slightly hooked, shallow face, with the whip in the last ten inches of the shaft – exactly my specs. I can't wait to try it.'

'Might be tricky getting on the course this morning, m'dear. I have been trying my hand at the goff and I must admit that it makes a fair pastime. In fact, I've formed a club and I've just finished formulating the constitution. Would you like me to read it?'

The Queen's eyes narrowed and she replied quietly between clenched teeth: 'Just read the bits which mean that the Queen of Scotland might find it a bit tricky to play goff on her own course.'

'Ah. That comes under the heading of Rights and Privileges of Non-Voting Members. Here we go: "Non-voting members shall pay concessionary dues and in return shall enjoy full playing privileges on the course after 6 p.m., except during the summer months, and shall otherwise have the full benefit of playing privileges provided that they vacate the course by 8.30 a.m. In order that the sensibilities of the non-voting members shall not be offended by the coarse behaviour and vulgar language of the full members, the non-voting members shall have their own separate clubhouse accommodation . . .".'

'Wait! Where are these separate clubhouse quarters?'

'Ah. We've done up the old mule stable, whitewashed throughout and equipped with a bucket and basin with a stoup of water. Mistress Nicol has made a delightful cover for the bucket with a pretty chintz frill. Now, where was I? Oh yes, "Non-voting members shall in no circumstances enter the full members' clubhouse, nor linger in front of the steps, nor wear trews on the course, nor address the full members, nor in any manner desport themselves in such manner as to cause offence to the full members." Not a bad deal, eh? After all, you will get your goff for a mere seventy shillings a year.'

At this moment the Earl of Bothwell entered. The Queen cut short his greetings with an imperious wave of her hand. 'My Lord Bothwell, you arrive at a most opportune time. My Lord Darnley has committed gross treason against your sovereign lady, the Queen. Strangle the bastard.'

She rose and strode quickly from the room, not quite quickly enough to avoid the sound of a scuffle and curious gurgling noises. She grabbed her clubs and proceeded out of the house into the grounds. The first object which caught her eye was a notice reading: 'Seton Place Golf and Country Club. No dogs, no women.'

The Queen followed the path down to the dower house which, as she observed with anger, was adorned with a flag bearing the legend SPGC.

13

'She was pondering a cut-up cleek over the burn at the fourth hole . . .'

Brandishing her trusty niblick she brushed aside the cowering flunkey at the door and entered the great hall. Various noblemen were lounging around, engaged in loud talk and hearty laughter. She caught a scrap of conversation: '. . . after he was arraigned by the Cardinal for failing to consummate the marriage he entered a defence but he couldn't make it stand up in the ecclesiastical court.' The guffaw which greeted this sally was cut short by the Queen's curt command: 'Out, out, you poxy villains!' There was a stampede for the door, and now the Queen saw at the end of the room a table behind which stood a servant dispensing twenty-five brands of mead, all on the optic. With one sweep of her niblick she smashed the bottles, and the terrified serf dived to safety through the window. All was silence. The Queen walked slowly to the first tee, summoning her cadet to follow with her clubs.

She was pondering a cut-up cleek over the burn at the fourth hole, or possibly a lay-up with the mashie, when Lord Bothwell approached at a run. 'Hold your hand, ma'am,' he called. A great explosion knocked them both to the ground. Fragments of brick and timber fell around them.

'You have blown up my house,' she accused.

'Quite so, your majesty. Evidence. Couldn't risk leaving any clues.'

'You are probably right,' said the Queen. 'Dear Bothwell, you think of everything.'

She held out her hand. He took it gently. 'I wanted to be sure that you were not at the top of your backswing when the bang went off,' said Bothwell.

'So considerate,' said the Queen, squeezing his hand. 'You know, that brute Darnley even had the nerve to suggest that you looked at me with unseemly boldness.'

'Heaven forbid, my lady, though 'tis true that you are exceedingly comely, lying there on the verdant turf with those coaxing hemispheres heaving beneath thine bodice. No more loyal subject draws breath throughout thine fiefdom, ma'am, but verily your humble servant is not made of wood.'

The Queen laughed prettily: 'From the heaving of your cod-piece, Master Bothwell, you are indeed made of wood.'

Shortly afterwards they were married, but wagging tongues created such a scandal of innuendo that the Queen was imprisoned and forced to

15

abdicate. She escaped to the sanctuary of England since she was the natural heir to Queen Elizabeth. So much for family ties: Elizabeth put her back into prison.

Meanwhile a former kitchen porter at Seton Place was working his way slowly towards London. This man, one Auchterlonie, had just entered the breakfast room to clear the dishes when the explosion occurred. He was blown through the window and his fall was luckily broken by the branches of a tall mountain ash. When he recovered his senses he climbed down and on the ground he found a parchment, slightly singed but otherwise complete. Auchterlonie could not read, but with native cunning he folded the parchment and tucked it safely into his sporran in the hope that it might prove valuable.

His first priority must be to escape from the scene of devastation as quickly as possible, lest he be implicated in the murder of his master. He sheltered in a dense beech wood, and next morning he fell in with an itinerant turner who eked out a precarious living by making wooden golf balls.

'Exports. That's the thing,' said Auchterlonie to the turner. 'You'll never amount to anything unless you expand your market. Tell you what. You give me a sack of golf balls and I will be your rep. They're playing golf in England these days and I'll open up the territory.'

'But surely they turn their own golf balls down in England,' objected the turner.

'Aye, but Scotland's got the reputation. Golfers will pay anything for equipment made in Scotland.'

The turner agreed and worked with a will. Auchterlonie took his sack and found a cleric with a weakness for usquebaugh who painstakingly marked each ball with the legend: 'Warranted hand-made in St Andrews. 100 compression.'

Auchterlonie prospered on his journeying through England, picking up the rudiments of civilized behaviour as he reached the southern counties. He settled at Blackheath, forming a business to import leather balls stuffed with uncombed lambswool from the Low Countries, and soon he had won a reputation among the gentry as a sharp but essentially honest tradesman. In this manner he struck up a friendship with one of his regular customers, William Cecil, first minister to Queen Elizabeth.

One day when Cecil was visiting the shop of Auchterlonie, the former kitchen porter brought out the parchment and said: 'By the way, noble sir, as a collector of golfing memorabilia you might be interested in this. It is from the home of that great golfing pioneer, Lord Darnley, who, as you know, was foully murdered some years since.'

Cecil read the parchment with interest. 'Gad! But this is good stuff, enlightened in that it recognizes a place for women in golf but pragmatically liberal in its understanding of women's proper place in the natural order of things. The sentiments remind me of my old friend John Knox's essay on "The first blast of the trumpet against the monstrous regiment of women". Women have their place, and it is an important place, but they must be kept in their place. And you say that the bitch Mary had Darnley murdered because of this perfectly conceived golf club constitution?'

'So 'twas said,' replied Auchterlonie.

'And she wrecked the joint?'

'That was the story in East Lothian, sire.'

'Just as well she is safely in prison,' said Cecil.

'In prison, yes, but I don't know so much about safely. She escaped from prison in Scotland.'

'So she did. What would happen if she escaped again and got up to her old tricks of causing trouble at golf clubs? She has to be stopped! Leave this to me, Auchterlonie, and say nothing to anybody about this conversation.'

The following day the Chief Minister of State had his regular audience with Queen Elizabeth. She was impatient for news about the war with Spain.

'It's going rather well, ma'am. We have received intelligence that Sir Francis Drake has had a great victory at Cadiz. One gathers that the Spanish fleet was pretty well destroyed. The Treasury is getting agitated about the cost of all these wars, but they are always agitated about something. By the way, we have unearthed a Papist plot against your life, your majesty, and I am sorry to tell you that Mary Queen of Scots is behind it!'

'But Mary's in the Tower.'

'Exactly, ma'am, but she is the focus of a brewing rebellion. My advice is to nip it in the bud.'

'What do you suggest?'

Cecil made a chopping motion with his open hand.

'Very well. See to it, will you?'

Thus it was that the first woman golfer met her just deserts and the game was preserved for centuries to come.

4
Golf Loses Its Feathers

As every student of golf knows because it was all explained in Chapter 2, in the year 1457 King James II of Scotland decreed that 'ye futeball and ye golfe and ither sich unprofitable sports be utterlie cryit doune and nicht be usit in all ye realme'. Some forty years later his grandson, James IV, decreed: 'It is statute and ordained that in na place of the Realme there be used fute-ball, golfe and ither sik unprofitable sports.'

The reason for these prohibitions was because the citizens were neglecting their archery practice. The nation of golf nuts took exception to this royal interference and utterlie cryed downe the Stuart kings for neglecting their spelling lessons.

Titanic Thompson is generally credited with being golf's first con-artist, but in truth the tradition of dirty tricks goes back many centuries. In 1681 the Duke of York had an argument with two English noblemen, both hot-shot players, and the Duke threw down a challenge: 'Me and my caddie could beat your brains out the best day you ever had.' The nobles answered: 'Put up the bread and let's go.'

The Duke sent for the local champion, a shoemaker called John Patersone, and instructed him to keep his trap shut and his long putts up to the hole. With the help of this ringer the Duke took the two pigeons to the cleaners, and this match is believed to be the origin of the popular golf expletive 'Cobblers'.

By that time the featherie ball had come into golf, a vast improvement on the old wooden balls but much more expensive. One ball cost a week's wages for a labourer and golf became a rich man's game. All that changed when Dr Paterson of St Andrews University received a package sent by a

'He pulled it off and idly rolled the soft gutta percha into a ball.'

waggish friend from Singapore. It was an erotic statue of Vishnu engaged in a Hindu fertility rite with two temple maidens and it was moulded from gutta percha, a resin similar to latex which hardens on exposure to the air.

Dr Paterson was chuckling over the wild improbability of the proportions of this vulgar objet d'art when his wife entered the study. She shrieked with horror, picked up the obscenity and hurled it into the fire before flouncing out to have a fit of the vapours in the comfort of her boudoir. Dr Paterson took the fire tongs and retrieved his gift but by now the heat had reduced it to the consistency of putty, its form grotesquely distorted with the giant phallus sadly drooping. He pulled it off and idly rolled the soft gutta percha into a ball.

Overnight the ball hardened and Dr Paterson mused: 'I wonder. . . .' Grabbing his cleek he hurried to the links and struck the ball. It made a satisfying click as he caught it on the meat of the club but the ball went nowhere, dipping abruptly in the air and rolling to a halt.

His experiment was watched by a fanatical golfer known to one and all as Ankleball Mackenzie because of his inability to get his shots into the air. Mackenzie was waiting to tee off in the monthly medal and begged to try a shot with this novel ball. 'Here, you can have the bloody thing,' said Dr Paterson. Ankleball played the first four holes in a series of scuffing half-tops, by which time the ball was sadly scarred from its maltreatment and his score stood at 58. Normally it was about here that he tore up his card, but by happy chance he was playing with the redoubtable Monsieur Samuel Messieux, French master at Madras College and a considerable player who had once driven a featherie a measured 361 yards.

'Holy blue!' said M. Messieux, 'but your golf is *insupportable. Ecoute.* Imagine, *mon brave,* that on every *coup* your ball is on a tee, not a proper sand tee, *comprenez,* but a *petit* piece of wood like a peg. Now forget about ze ball and try to *coupez* that peg *imaginaire* under ze ball.'

'You mean like this?' said Ankleball, getting the blade to the bottom of the ball for the first time in his life. To his astonishment the ball rose and soared and finally pitched four yards past the flag at the unprecedented distance in Ankleball's experience of 180 yards, taking one hop and spinning back to the lip of the cup.

'Bravo!' said Monsieur Messieux.

'It's a miracle,' said Ankleball. He completed the remaining holes in level fours and headed straight for the bar. 'This calls for a celebration,' he cried, so far forgetting himself in the excitement as to add: 'The drinks are on me.' The streets of St Andrews emptied. True to the time-honoured practices of his calling, the barman soon judged the time to be propitious to unload some of his old stock. He had a number of bottles of foreign muck which had been gathering dust for years and he laced the whisky liberally.

There's always one. A latecomer whose palate had not become fully anaesthetized by neat Scotch asked crossly: 'What in Hades is this? It's nae bad but it's nae a dram.' Apart from a talent for swindling the landlord a barman's greatest asset is the ability to come up with a plausible falsehood at short notice. ''Tis a special concoction I have devised to celebrate a notable milestone on the glorious road of golf. I call it an Ankleball.'

'Nay,' interjected Mackenzie. 'That name died for ever on the Ginger Beer hole. This drink must be called a Highball.'

Alone in St Andrews one man was not celebrating. Allan Robertson, the champion of champions, had observed the phenomenon of the gutta percha ball on the links and he sat alone in the Union Parlour bar, sulking over his dram and deep in thought. He had six men working full time at the bench making featherie balls. His business would be ruined. Maybe he could corner the gutta percha market and kill this new invention. No, that wouldn't work. The expense would be prohibitive. The same went for bribing the Implements and Balls committee to ban the new ball. There was only one answer.

He hurried back to his workshop, parcelled up every featherie ball in the place and despatched them to his regular customers with a covering letter. 'In view of the seasonal shortage of goose down feathers and an inevitable rise in costs, I am favouring my loyal customers with a twelve-month priority supply of first-grade golf balls at the old price. Prompt payment will be appreciated. Assuring you of my continued consideration at all times. Yours faithfully, A. Robertson.'

He then walked round the corner to the blacksmith's shop and sketched a design in the soot on the apprentice's forehead. 'See here, Hamish, I want you to make me a ball mould in two parts, with a bramble pattern.' He just had time to catch the chief clerk at the Oriental Supply and Import Company to put in his order for the immediate shipment of 10 cwt best gutta percha. As usual, Allan Robertson was ahead of the game.

This was literally true. Thanks to mysterious injuries which defied medical science whenever he received a challenge from Willie Park, Robertson was able to sustain his proud boast that he had never been beaten in a level match.

His untimely death therefore raised a question about a successor to the throne of the uncrowned king of golf. The Earl of Eglington had an idea and made a proposal to his fellow golfers at Prestwick. There could be no question of allowing these rude fellows to compete in the championship, of course, but it might be amusing to let those professional chappies play each other in a small sideshow. 'We could call it a General Golf Competition for Scotland. I know there is a danger of them getting uppity, so just to remind them of their station in life as servants I suggest they be made to wear the livery of my estate staff.'

The members agreed that this was a capital idea and the tournament went ahead. It was such a success they did it again the following year, only this time they relaxed the conditions of entry and called it the Open championship.

5

St Andrews Takes the Lead

In the prim moral climate of today Kate McCurdie would be described as no better than she should be. Minds were broader in the middle of the eighteenth century and, while there may have been some scandalized whispering behind prayer books by a few matrons, for the most part Kate was well respected in St Andrews. Perhaps it would be truer to say that she was respectfully treated by the city dignitaries because they knew that she knew and that made her a walking time-bomb.

The secret of Kate's success was that she learnt early in her career that men like to drink when they are happy or sad and that, furthermore, the drink made them feel amorous, a condition which also obtained without benefit of drink. She thus became a camp follower during the '45 rebellion and did good business among the troops of both sides at the battles of Prestonpans and Culloden, subsequently following Prince Charlie into exile in France where she picked up some useful hints on advanced technique.

She was therefore able on returning to her native land to purchase a substantial building on the outskirts of the city and furnish it as an inn. Kate McCurdie's tavern was the first hostelry which travellers met on their journeys to St Andrews, which is why she chose this location of course, but she soon discovered that the men who hit wooden balls over the common land along the seashore worked up tremendous thirsts at their strange pursuit. They liked to come into her parlour and quaff vast quantities of ale while they told each other lies about how well they had played and what ill fortune they had suffered.

One day a group of these golfers approached Kate and enquired if they might hire a private room one evening a week in which to assemble and dine. 'How private?' asked Kate.

'Oh, extremely private,' they said.

'Do you mean so private that it would be indiscreet to allow local serving wenches to wait at the table? You know how everybody knows everybody else in a small community and how tongues wag.'

'Good gracious, Kate, what a perceptive woman you are,' replied the golfers. 'But what do you suggest?'

'I had in mind to bring in outsiders,' said Kate, 'possibly from Dundee or Edinburgh. They could travel in a closed coach. If we can arrange satisfactory terms I am sure I could find suitable girls, young, beautiful and of accommodating nature.'

'That sounds splendid,' said the golfers, 'but do you have a room which would guarantee our privacy?'

'I could do out the cellar,' said Kate. 'You would even have your own entrance, through the side door in the alley and down the back stairs. Nobody would even know you were in the building; these stone floors are so thick that you could hold an orgy down there and nobody would hear a thing.'

The golfers laughed excitedly. 'What a card you are to be sure, Mistress Kate. An orgy indeed! And all of us pillars of society! The very idea!'

'I am not completely unfamiliar with the ways of society,' replied Kate, 'nor its pillars.'

One of the golfers who seemed to be their leader raised his hand to silence the guffaws. 'You say that none of your customers would even know that we were here. Well, it is essential that we have privacy but it is also important that it shall be known to our friends and our good wives that this is our meeting place. We want privacy but not total secrecy, if you take the distinction.'

Kate winked. 'I once encountered a similar problem with the dining club of a French cavalry regiment. If you will return this evening after sunset I shall show you how your dilemma might be solved.'

The golfers agreed, and that evening they duly entered Kate McCurdie's tavern agog to know what stratagem she had planned.

'Follow me, please, gentlemen,' said Kate, leading the way into the street. 'What do you see up there?' she asked, indicating an upstairs window. On the blinds they observed the shadow of diners seated at table.

'Do you see any wenches bearing foaming tankards?' asked Kate, 'or any lewd behaviour? Or an orgy?'

'Not at all,' said the leader of the golfers. 'They seem to be a very sober crowd, apparently engaged in discourse of a most serious nature to judge by their quiet demeanour. Surely you have not engaged the services of strolling players to impersonate us? We are generous men and willing to pay well for our pleasures, but the hiring of many actors would surely be beyond our means.'

'Come and see,' said Kate, leading the procession into the inn and up the stairs, past a prominent notice reading 'Private function. Society of St Andrews Goffers. Strictly members only.' Inside the room was a long table with chairs ranged alongside and on each chair was strapped a dummy upper body made of old clothes packed with heather. A guttering candle set in a draught threw flickering shadows of the scene onto the blinds, giving the impression of animation.

'Scarecrows!' said one of the goffers in admiration.

'Pure genius, Kate,' said the leader. 'We are just a bunch of stuffed shirts.'

So was born the Society of St Andrews Golfers and for many a year, for the price of a penny candle, the members revelled in drunken lewdness in the cellar while gaining a growing reputation as the most respectable and sober sportsmen in the land.

The word spread. The scandals which attended the raffish behaviour of the golfers of Leith and Prestwick served only to add to the candlepower of the haloes of the St Andrews Society. The world assumed that the proximity of the cathedral must have a sanctifying effect on the golfers of the Eden estuary since they were so dedicated to golf that all they ever did was play and then sit over a quiet weekly dinner and discuss such weighty matters as the morality of the stymie, the legal dilemma of the plugged ball and the merits of a straight left arm.

Then one evening, when the weekly dinner was particularly well attended because it was the leader's birthday, four scantily dressed wenches entered the cellar pushing a cart on which sat an enormous cake. The wenches sang: 'Here's something to tickle your fancy, darling Bill / And if she doesn't then one of us will' at which the cake erupted in a volcano of confectionery and out popped a naked girl who trilled: 'Happy Birthday, Mr Captain. By the way, this came for you in the post. I expect it's a card.'

26

'By the way, this came for you in the post.'

The Captain opened the envelope and as he read the letter his face grew serious. 'Gentlemen, listen to this. "We, the undermentioned Societies, being desirous of promoting the welfare of the ancient and healthful sport of golf, request and beseech the noble Society of St Andrews Golfers in its wisdom and propriety to assume the government of the said sport and in particular to bring an end to the conflict which exists through differing codes of rules obtaining within individual societies and to draw up one universal code of laws to which all golfers shall be solemnly bound. We pledge our loyalty to the Society of St Andrews Golfers whose seemly and upright character is an example to us all."'

From the back of the room the unmistakable hellfire and damnation voice of Deacon Sime growled: 'There's only one rule of golf. Hit it, find it, and hit it again.'

'We know that,' said the Captain, 'but they have included copies of all their rules. Edinburgh has thirteen rules, for instance, and listen to this: "Your tee must be upon the ground" whatever that means.'

'It means,' said old Walkinshaw, 'that you have to spell out every last detail to an Edinburgh man as if to a backward child.'

'Then there's something about watery filth,' said the Captain.

'Talking of watery filth, Mr Captain,' shouted Bailie Sutherland, 'could you prevail on Mistress Kate to stop whatever she is doing with that lecherous Sutherland and fetch us another hogshead of claret?'

'Order! Order!' shouted the Captain. 'Can I have a sensible proposition about what we should do in this matter?'

Dominie Grant rose and held up his hand for silence. 'I move that this letter be lain on the table alongside the Captain and his birthday present.' The proposition was carried by acclaim and normal revelries were resumed.

The letter was placed on the table upstairs and there it stayed, growing yellow among the stuffed shirts, until Kate died seven years later. The game was clearly up, and a group of mourning members climbed the tavern stairs to remove the tableau which had put such a respectable face on the nocturnal revels for so long. The dust was blown from the forgotten letter.

'We'd better do something about this, I suppose,' said one.

'Might as well,' said another, the one named Cheape. 'After all, we won't have anything else to occupy our time now that Kate's tavern is finished. But I tell you what: the good times may be over for the time being but they will be back.'

'No chance,' said the first member. 'Once we take over the administration of golf the gaze of the world will be upon us and if one of us so much as looks at a woman, or takes a dram, it will be all over the papers.'

'Don't worry,' said Cheape, 'one day we'll have our own place, somewhere quiet, maybe down by the beach.'

6
America Hears the Call

Doctor Grace was in good form with the bat. British expeditionary forces were slaughtering insurgents of various pigments in satisfactory numbers in distant lands. Queen Victoria was on the throne, the jute market was firm, God was in his heaven and all was right with the world. In short, there was nothing to disturb the equanimity of the four R & A members who took their brandy and cigars into the Big Room after lunch and sank contentedly into the deep leather chairs by the window. Within minutes they were snoring in four-part harmony.

They were awakened by a noise which skewered them like an electric cattle prod.

'WHOOPEE!'

The cry seemed to originate from somewhere beyond the railway sheds, perhaps the 16th green or 17th tee.

'Good Lord, somebody's being murdered.'

'WAY TO GO, PRO!'

'They can't be sticking a pig; that's human speech – almost.'

'GREAT SHOT, TOMMY BABY!'

The volume was increasing, something which the four members would have wagered to be impossible for unaided vocal chords to achieve.

'GET IN THE HOLE!'

Sir Angus Farquahar of That Ilk reached out a palsied hand and tugged at the bell cord. The club retainer entered.

'Ah, MacWhistlebreeches, who the devil is making all that din?'

'That is Mr Macdonald, sir,' replied the servant, adding by way of explanation, 'an American gentleman.'

'AWESOME, MAN, AWESOME!'

'Is he a member?'

'Indeed, yes.'

'ONE TIME!'

By now the window panes were audibly rattling at each verbal on-slaught.

'HOT DIGGITY DAWG!'

'Something's got to be done about this bounder. Anybody got a horse whip?'

'Hang on, Angus,' said Baron Cupar of Cupar. 'We don't want a diplo-matic incident. Remember, America's a good export market.'

'No shop in the club, Cupar of Cupar,' said the Earl of Anstruther.

'Sorry,' said the Baron, 'it's my shout for the next round. Got a bit carried away. But this thing will have to be handled in a statesmanlike manner. . . .'

'GODDAMN WE SKINNED 'EM!'

'. . . Balfour's our man, devious devil like all politicians. Got to go to town to see him, anyway. I'll get him on to it.'

'DID WE EVER SKIN THESE TURKEYS?'

'Don't waste any time,' said Sir Angus.

Arthur Balfour greeted his old friend in the dining room at the House of Commons.

'What can I do for you?'

'Two things, actually. About this place we've just annexed in Africa. . . .'

'Sierra Leone?'

'No, begins with a B. Baluchistan? Bessarabia?'

'You mean Bechuanalar ⌐ What about it?'

'The jute market. Any chai ⌐ ⌐ etting in on the ground floor?'

'There might be. What was the other thing you wanted to talk about?'

'Ah! It's this frightful chap Macdonald at the club. Shouts and screams. Turns the course into bedlam. It's quite intolerable. He'll be wearing two-tone shoes next, and chewing gum, I shouldn't wonder. He's got to be stopped.'

31

Balfour paled. 'I'll get onto it straight away. You will excuse me but obviously this is an urgent matter.'

The cabinet minister hurried off to his office and glanced at the papers in his despatch box. Top-priority demand from Lord Kitchener for reinforcements to be rushed to the Sudan. Memo marked 'Action this day' in the Prime Minister's hand about some clown called Jameson who had disobeyed explicit orders and stirred up the Boers to rebellion in the Transvaal. Surgeon General's report on outbreak of beri-beri among the troops fighting the Ashanti. Ambassador's report on trouble brewing in China.

Nothing that can't wait, thought Balfour, as he hurried out of the Palace of Westminster and hailed a cab. 'St Pancras Station and quick about it.'

'My dear Mr Macdonald, or may I call you Charles? I cannot tell you how happy we are to have one of our American cousins here at St Andrews. I gather you've done frightfully well at the university and, of course, your prowess at our game of golf is a byword within the game. Morris speaks most highly of your approach play. Obviously you have a glittering future in both your career and in sport. May I ask what line of commerce or profession you intend to pursue? The family business back in Chicago, perhaps?'

'No sir!' replied the sturdy youth. 'This is where it's at. I'm going to spend the rest of my days right here in Snanders.'

'St Andrews?'

'Yessir! And I figure I'll play the Old Course every day until I die.'

'Really! That's most interesting, although my friends in Yonkers will be disappointed to hear of your decision. Still, it's your life.'

'Yonkers? Why should your friends give a damn what I do for a living?'

'Oh, it was just a thought. These friends have made a golf course and rather sportingly they want to introduce the American people to the pleasures of our quaint little game. The problem is that they don't know the first thing about golf. Oh, they know that you have to hit the ball with a club but the subtleties, the etiquette, the niceties and traditions of golf and club life – these things are a closed book to them. I can send a professional over to teach them the rudiments of play but, as you know, these rough fellows are totally unsuitable as missionaries for what I may presume to call the golfing way of life. When I think of what your country-men have done to cricket and rugby football I must say that I fear for the future of golf in the United States. Coloured golf balls? Women members? Drivers made of metal? Motor cars to drive around the course? Who knows which way the game might go without expert guidance?'

'You couldn't play golf in a motor car!'

'You never know. And it would be such a pity if their ignorant blundering were to lead them into innovations which detracted from the pleasures of the game. I must confess that I harboured a secret hope that someone thoroughly versed in the true way of golf, someone who could speak to them in their own language, could take control of this infant American game and direct its footsteps along the path of righteousness.'

'Someone like *me*? But I'm fresh out of school.'

'A wise old head on sturdy young shoulders, my dear Charles, the perfect credentials for such a mission. Just think, because of your unique qualifications you would return to your homeland as a Messiah. You would be the king of golf, the unchallenged ruler of the game throughout the New World. You would be the Royal and Ancient club embodied in one man. What a challenge – and what an opportunity!'

'I could never be the Royal and Ancient, Mr Balfour. America's a republic; they wouldn't stand still for any royal crap.'

'An astute point, Charles. But you could be president. Yes, president of the Democratic Society of American Golfers. How does that sound?'

'I'm not sure about the democratic bit. I like to get my own way without a bunch of voters telling me what to do. How about president of the United States Golf Association?'

'Perfect!'

'Goddamn, I'll do it!'

'I'm so glad, absolutely delighted. Here, I've taken the liberty in antici-pation of your public-spirited acceptance of booking you a ticket on the next packet. It sails tonight from Liverpool.'

That evening Lord Cupar approached Arthur Balfour in the Big Room after dinner.

'. . . I've taken the liberty of booking you a ticket on the next packet.'

'Have you settled the hash of the human foghorn, Arthur?'

Balfour gazed at the ceiling. 'May America forgive me for what I have done. By the way, Cupar, I'm afraid it's no go about Bechuanaland. Apparently, they don't eat jute.'

7
How the Ball Got Its Bounce

Little research, if indeed any, has been undertaken into the relationship between golf and dentistry, probably because sociologists are not interested in the game, being too busy devising complicated experiments to prove what the rest of us know perfectly well from sheer common sense. Once they are into a programme of analysing the diets of juvenile Bolivian rag-pickers, correlating calorific values against body weight and then writing incomprehensible reports documenting a tendency to physical underdevelopment among the malnourished, they have little time for outdoor pursuits.

The average golf club membership contains two dentists, a statistically insignificant sample, and so the other members do not find it remarkable that they both play to single figures. It could be coincidence. Of course the dentists get ribbed about having strong hands from all those hours of yanking teeth, but that is as far as it goes.

But if that happens in every club, as we all know it does, then the global picture reveals a remarkable picture: every golfing dentist in the universe plays to a handicap of 9 or better. Obviously there must be more to it than wiry wrists, otherwise lumberjacks would win all the monthly medals.

Let us examine the facts. Dentistry is a job within a job – the violent physical exertion of extracting an impacted molar combined with the delicate artistry of drilling out a cavity, an exact parallel with golf's *Sturm und Drang* of the long game and the gentle precision of putting.

Furthermore, the nature of dentistry conditions its practitioners in the patience, serenity and low cunning which are the very qualities needed for golf. Doctors, architects, accountants, captains of industry and shop keepers are unsuited to golf because they are neurotic if not downright paranoid.

They are prey to constant worries about patients bringing malpractice suits, foundations crumbling, auditors turning up evidence of cooked books, revolts by stockholders and staff pilfering the merchandise. But the dentist does not have a care in the world. If he should make a mistake, and they are subject to normal human failings, he has the remedy at hand. When his hand slips he inspects the devastation in his little mirror, puts on his expression of concern and remarks: 'Pity we didn't get to this one sooner. I just hope we're not too late to save the tooth.' A simple filling has thus been elevated to a course of six treatments, with X-rays, until finally he whips out the evidence of his incompetence, holds it up with the forceps and remarks: 'There! That little beggar won't give you any more trouble.' Depending on whether or not the tooth has a gold filling it is then consigned to the bin or the crucible. The patient pays and departs, free of pain, guaranteed to return for lucrative bridge work, and impressed with the patience and infinite trouble the dentist has expended on trying to save the tooth.

Dr Cary Middleroff was the patron saint of golfing dentists, an artist who would have won even more championships but for his surgery habit of spinning out his appointments by pausing in deep professional contemplation for minutes on end before reaching for the appropriate instrument. 'Number eight iron, please nurse.'

Another link between golf and dentistry is, of course, gutta percha, widely used as a temporary filling, and it was this substance which formed the subject of conversation between Coburn Haskell and his dentist one day in Cleveland, Ohio, towards the end of the nineteenth century.

'I'll just plug this hole with gutta percha,' said the dentist. 'That's the stuff they make golf balls with. Wonderful game. Do you play?'

'Urr hoo row ha arrgh,' replied Haskell.

'Capital,' said the dentist. 'We must have a game some time. What line of work are you in?'

'Or hoy hurrah nor wow vowoh.'

'An inventor, eh? I wish you'd invent a decent golf ball that I could fly 240 with the driver.'

In fact Haskell had been pondering deeply on quite a different problem. As he lay back he observed through tear-filled eyes the blurred mechanics

'. . . I just hope we're not too late to save the tooth.'

of the dentist's foot-treadle drill and his inventive resources were urgently directed on improvements, something less noisy and – above all – less painful.

'Pity we didn't get to this sooner. I just hope we're in time to save the tooth. Make an appointment with the receptionist for another treatment tomorrow,' said the dentist.

Haskell returned to his bicycle factory and went straight to his drawing board in the research and development office.

The Haskell Patented Dental Drill never came to anything, but the prototype showed definite promise. He invited his dentist to inspect it.

The dentist seated himself on the saddle and pedalled furiously, brandishing the flexible drill lead above his head in the manner of a rodeo rider. By one of those unhappy, or happy, chances by which the destiny of great enterprises has so often turned, a bicycle inner tube chose this moment to drop from an overhead rack and entangle itself in the whirring gear wheels of the prototype drill. The machinery reduced the rubber tube to fine shreds which was carried along the chain and caught up between two cogs where it wound itself, being under tension, into a tight ball.

'You've done it, man. You've done it!' cried the dentist. 'Put a resilient cover on that and you've got a perfect golf ball.'

And so it was done. The dentist won the club's long driving competition that weekend and the man he beat, B. F. Goodrich, hurried off for urgent discussions with Coburn Haskell.

The most important development in the history of golf, the rubber core ball, was born and the Goodrich Rubber company of Akron, Ohio, went into production.

In Britain the golfers were outraged by this Yankee 'Bounding Billy', and anyone who forsook the guttie for the lively new ball was condemned as a bounder. The professionals, whose living depended largely on the making and selling of gutties, were forthright in their scathing criticism, none more so than Sandy Herd. 'It's nae goof, nae goof at all,' growled Herd, slipping one into his pocket.

He, alone, played a Haskell in the Open championship, which naturally he won. Golf had entered a new era.

8
How the Rules Got Into That State

When a man sits down to write his life story, always a mistake and almost as unfortunate as deciding to grow a moustache, he is tempted to show himself in as good a light as possible. That is human nature, and so there is a tendency to gloss over that episode with the Can Can dancer or to omit it entirely.

The history of golf suffers from the same selective process, since the early golf historians were invariably themselves pillars of the golfing establishment. No such charge could ever be levelled against this scholarly work whose integrity is beyond compromise. Thus, fearlessly searching for the truth no matter how unpalatable this may prove to be, some of the mysterious and clouded areas of the game must be subjected to the glare of public scrutiny.

Take the earliest-known written code of golf. There were only thirteen rules in the middle of the eighteenth century and one of those does not count because it is totally incomprehensible. Rule 2 stated: 'Your tee must be upon the ground.' It is admirably succinct, if meaningless, and historians have always swept that rule under the carpet, blandly remarking that while it may be obscure to contemporary golfers it probably had some validity at the time.

After years of patient research in the dusty municipal archives of Scotland, and many hours crawling around dank cemeteries deciphering the inscriptions on tomb stones, a massive body of evidence was uncovered about fatalities incurred by 'ane straik on the lug (ear) by ane golfe clubbe'. The number of such deaths was far too high to be explained by simple accident. There had to be a reason, and diligent probing eventually revealed it – although, unfortunately, the real name of the culprit still eludes detection.

He is simply referred to, in the tavern songs of the period, as the Black Abbot. The common golfing expletive 'Holy shit!' undoubtedly derives from the Black Abbot because that is the nickname by which he is identified in several dirges, as in the refrain:

Dinna hang doun yer heid, Tam Dooley, 'ere the holy shite swings,
Lest ye swap yeir nut for a pair o' angel's wings.

The Abbot was a portly man and a touch of arthritis in the lower back further restricted his capacity to wield a golf club. Such was his enthusiasm for the game, however, that nothing would deter him from his daily excursion on the links. To facilitate a full shoulder turn he adopted the habit of teeing his ball on top of his caddie's head. Make that a succession of caddies, for he inflicted dreadful carnage among the youth of Musselburgh.

The sanctity of his cloth preserved him from the prying attention of the authorities for a while, but the scandal could not be delayed indefinitely. The bishop got to hear about it and the Black Abbot was confined to his cell, although the story was hushed up by the usual conspiracy of silence when a dignitary falls from grace. Without the solace of his golf the Abbot pined and soon fell into a mortal sleep. He was buried in an unmarked grave, although they did observe his last wish and alongside him in the grave they laid his driver, Auld Lobotomizer.

The golf establishment was well aware of the Black Abbot's idiosyncrasy. He had quite a reputation because when he really nailed one – the ball, not the caddie – he hit some massive drives. Other golfers seriously considered adopting the old cleric's method.

There was nothing for it but to frame a rule insisting that the tee be on the ground, and we can see how much importance was attached to this condition by the fact that this was the second rule of golf.

Another mystery from those original laws occurs in the casual water rule because of the expression 'or watery filth'. The records of the Edinburgh Court of Session provide the vital clue with the conviction and banishment to the outer isles of one MacVicar for purveying adulterated claret to the Honourable Company of Edinburgh Golfers. A club minute relates that the members very properly and in high anger disposed of this watery filth

'Rule 2 stated: Your tee must be upon the ground.'

on the golf course without previous benefit of imbibing and micturition. Today we would call this a temporary local rule.

The mystery which continues to elude researchers is the identity of the golfer who inspired the frenzied proliferation of the rules. Within the space of a hundred years the rules grew from a few scribbled notes such as could easily be accommodated on a postcard to two volumes of Definitions, Rules, Appendices and Decision which together involve a mass of verbiage weighing in excess of five pounds.

The original rules assumed a high standard of sportsmanship, and reinforced this tacit understanding with such exhortations as 'You must play honestly at the hole'. Everyone understood and observed the sporting ethic, and so there was no need to spell out a prohibition against nudging your ball onto a convenient tuffet with the toe of your boot. But, obviously, somebody came along who was intent on pulling every dirty and devious trick in the book.

We can deduce a few facts about this vile creature. He was a good player, scratch or better, because the rules are expressly framed for good players. No matter that 99 per cent of golfers are, to a greater or lesser degree, choppers. The whole thrust of the rules is directed at the hot shots, as we can see from the lofty attitude of ignoring handicaps. In the hierarchy of golf, handicap golfers are peasants and the lawmakers do not deign to recognize their existence. It does not matter what they get up to, and if they want handicaps let them organize them amongst themselves.

It is also clear that our miscreant was an amateur, since the rules are obsessive about amateur status and the only mention of professionals is in derogatory terms, clearly inferring that they are beyond the pale. The amateur who infringes the rules is cast into the outer darkness of pro-fessionalism.

In the days when all this rule making became a growth industry amateur golf was an exclusive pastime reserved for the well off, and in the natural order of things that meant decent family origins, decent school, decent university (or decent regiment in the case of the intellectually handi-capped). So we now have a rough portrait of the mystery golfer, talented, well born, well educated, wealthy and consumed by an uncontrollable urge to cheat.

We can visualize him smearing his club faces with illegal substances before a match, teeing up in front of the markers, jangling his loose change as his opponent starts his downswing, surreptitiously kicking his ball out of the rough, testing the surface of the bunker sand, blatantly asking for advice, refusing to divulge how many strokes he had played, and cutting a hole in his trouser pocket to facilitate the dropping of a spare ball in emergencies.

For all his trickery he did not win much and we may surmise that this was due to fear of physical injury upsetting his putting stroke. The scenario probably went something like this:

'Would you mind not positioning yourself so that your shadow falls across the line of my putt?'

'There's nothing in the rules about that. I can stand where I like.'

'Not unless you want a broken nose as soon as we get to the privacy of the locker room. By the way, you are due a black eye in any case for dropping your bag and stopping my last putt.'

'That was an accident.'

'You can tell your friends, if you have any, that your black eye was an accident.'

The word would get around. Every time he played, the Rules of Golf committee would go into emergency session to plug the latest loophole. The traditionalists on the committee opposed monkeying about with the rules. 'Everybody knows that you have to play the ball as it lies. Do we really have to spell out that this means as it lies before you have given it a hearty kick?' The young turks, mainly pedants from the legal profession, insisted that every conceivable possibility must be covered by a specific rule. 'Everyone knows the Ten Commandments, but society still needs the rule of temporal law. Playing the ball as it lies is not so much a law as a philosophy, and you cannot regulate a game on philosophical precepts. We must have proper laws, and that means masses and masses of exceptions, variations, subclauses and interpretations. Believe us, it is the only way.'

'But nobody will be able to master and remember such a preponderance of legislation.'

'Don't worry about that; we lawyers will know the rules and we will come down like a ton of bricks on the transgressors.'

'Even if they do not realize that they are transgressing?'

'Especially if they do not know. Ignorance of the law is no defence.'

'Well, it seems a pity. We all know how to observe a philosophical doctrine, but I defy any golfer to make head or tail of that new rule we decreed last week about taking relief from an immovable obstruction in a hazard. Still, we must not stand in the way of progress.'

And so it came to pass in the middle of the twenty-first century that during the presentation ceremony at the Open championship the chairman of the Rules of Golf committee ran forward, snatched the trophy from the winner's hands and announced: 'Following an examination of the grooves in this competitor's wedge one groove was found to be outside the 2 per cent tolerance of the permitted maximum .035 inches width and this competitor is accordingly disqualified under Rule 427–29 xiii(c) as defined in Volume III of the Shorter Rules of Golf approved by the Royal and Ancient Golf Club of St Andrews and the United States Golf Association.'

9

The Golden Ages of Golf

After 2000 years of a rigid caste system the British are uncomfortable if they are transplanted into a different stratum of society. The working-class man who makes good, moves into a big house in Virginia Water and joins Sunningdale has to play the part of being middle class and never gives a convincing performance. He knows that his new peers refer to him as a nouveau riche, common as dirt counter-jumper, and that makes him almost as unhappy as the loss of his erstwhile pleasures of racing pigeons, darts in the pub and faggots and mushy peas for supper. If he is young enough to have children, names them Jeremy and Samantha and gets them into the pony club then this new generation has a chance of assimilating into the middle class, but the parents are doomed to a life of misery.

Golf developed its caste system to the point of caricature. The club president and captain represented the aristocracy and were preferably genuine aristocrats in real life, with generals and admirals being voted into office in emergency in the less fashionable clubs. The members formed the upper class, with the secretary and chief steward as the middle class.

The working class consisted of the professional, greenkeeping staff and menials, followed, in the more enlightened clubs, by the untouchables, or lady members. This was the situation during golf's first golden age when professional golf was dominated by the Great Triumvirate. This remarkable threesome consisted of the dour and taciturn James Braid, the dour and taciturn J. H. Taylor and the dour and taciturn Harry Vardon. Ted Ray was just as good a player but he was bluff and hearty and never got a look in, being forced to go to America to win an Open championship. He did his best to fake being taciturn by keeping a pipe permanently clenched between his teeth, but all this achieved was to keep his heartiness swathed in smoke and falling sparks, like an ebullient volcano.

The Triumvirate took turns to win the Open and they cornered the market for a generation. Then Vardon pulled a fast one. He invented a proper golf swing to replace the clumsy lunge which had remained in fashion for 400 years. It was a sneaky trick and the others had no option but to copy the new style.

America inherited the British way of golf and enthusiastically adopted the convention of treating the womenfolk as a sub-species of humanity. All the native American instincts favoured accepting the professionals as equals, even heroes, but the professionals themselves would not hear of such familiarity. They knew their allotted station in life, being immigrant Scots. Of course, these sons of Fife and Lothian won the US Open with boring regularity until something happened which was to change the course of the game.

An unknown teenage amateur who worked as an assistant in a sports store beat the giants of golf, Vardon and Ray, in a play-off for the Open. America exploded with delight and the country went golf mad. Honours were heaped on Francis Ouimet, even to the extent in later years of very nearly appointing him to the Presidency of the USGA.

American inventive genius was focused on golf and developments followed with bewildering speed: the triple-decker club sandwich, the Nassau and automatic presses, two-tone shoes, world domination and the convention of cute spelling (Topflite, Aer-flo, Hol-Hi, Shil-lay-ly, etc.). The most important advance of all was the invention of the star system which Walter Hagen pioneered as a one-man business.

Walter began according to sound marketing principles, concentrating first on the packaging of the product – tailored white plus-twos and colourful silk shirts – and a catchy slogan: 'Who's going to be second?' His next move was to learn how to play golf and then he was in business, cleaning up with exhibition matches around the world and employing a manager to carry away the money in a suitcase. He made his packet in a hurry because he was astute enough to recognize that there would be thin pickings in the game once the young Bobby Jones hit his stride. After Hagen golf would never be the same again, particularly for the professionals who were drawn along in his slipstream into an elevated status in respectable society.

In Britain that process of emancipation was accelerated by an arrogant, opinionated and snobbish young man named Henry Cotton who, in the opinion of his fellow pros, should have had all that nonsense knocked out of him at school. Cotton's decision to become a golfer arose literally from his refusal to bend over and take his punishment like a man. When he was at Alleyn's School he fell foul of the cricket establishment, and when he declined to be chastised for his mutinous behaviour the sports master banned him from playing cricket. 'In that case I will play golf,' said Cotton, and did. He was rebellious and insisted on living life on his own terms, an anti-hero until he won three Open championships and made the quantum leap from standoffish pain in the neck to lovable Grand Old Man of British Golf. By refusing to conform to the servants' hall status of pro golf, mocking the system by lunching from a Fortnum & Mason hamper in his Rolls-Royce when denied access to the club house, Cotton further elevated the standing of professional golfers.

Tony Jacklin followed along the lucrative path which Cotton had hacked through the thicket of snobbery and prejudice, but America was where it was all happening. An ambitious young lawyer named Mark McCormack, showing a marked lack of originality in the best traditions of his profession, invented the Big Three. He started by inventing a household god in Arnold Palmer and then exploited the commercial possibilities in setting two iconoclasts to knock the deity off his pedestal. For this purpose McCormack chose two unlikely contenders, the massive Jack Nicklaus and the tiny Gary Player. Actually the composition of the Big Three was brilliant casting. Nicklaus was the classical 'heavy', the man the fans loved to hate, while the South African Player played the character parts.

Whenever two or three golfers were gathered together the conversation would sooner or later get around to the question: 'What made Gary Player like that?' For a time the popular theory was that the baby Player had been abandoned in the bush and suckled by a tigress. Inevitably some smarty-pants discredited that fanciful legend by pointing out that there are no tigers in Africa.

The titanic struggle for supremacy among these three outstanding golfers made compulsive drama for the new medium of television and fortunes for everybody. This was the second golden age of professional golf and, as everyone knows, the issue was decided in favour of Nicklaus, because he was bigger than Player and Palmer's trousers kept falling down. When that golden age reached its natural end the supremacy of golf was up for grabs. And the golfing world was inherited by men from distant lands who could not speak English: Severiano Ballesteros, Bernhard Langer and Greg Norman.

10
How Bobby Became Immortal

Perhaps the most significant individual in the long history of golf was Bobby Jones. At a time when the world was falling into the philistine grip of materialism he represented the solid, old-fashioned virtues of modesty, sportsmanship and playing the game for the game's sake. For years he was virtually invincible, and when he put aside his clubs he made massive contributions to the literature of the game, to golf course architecture and tournament administration. The Bobby Jones story is too well known to be repeated here. Besides, you can read it all in *The Bobby Jones Story*, available from any public library.

But what manner of man was he? The best witness as to that must be Jones himself, and an insight into his character and how he was guided onto the path of his remarkable destiny is provided by the following fragment in his own hand and never before published. The papers, clearly a rough draft, were discovered recently rolled into a tight ball and stuffed into the toe of a golf shoe. We can only surmise that the shoes had been much too big for the youthful Jones, probably old stock that the crafty Stewart Maiden had unloaded onto the trusting youngster.

By Bobby Jones

When I look back and reflect on such successes as I may have achieved in golf I am conscious that the honours and kind expressions of congratulation which I have received should really be shared with another. Without the guidance of Stewart Maiden it is certain that other names would have been

'We can only surmise that the shoes had been much too big. . .'

inscribed on the 120 trophies and thirty medals which came my way. We first met when my parents took a cottage hard by the Atlanta Athletic club for the summer vacation of 1907. Stewart had recently arrived from Carnoustie to replace his brother Jimmy as the club professional, and this austere and taciturn Scot made a profound impression on me. He spoke little and what he did say was incomprehensible but we struck up an immediate bond. At that time I was a sickly child, the result of a digestive disorder, and it amazes me to this day what Stewart saw in the spindle-legged seven-year-old who was brought to him for lessons.

For some reason I have the idea that Stewart had served as a soldier, possibly in the Boer War. He suffered from some bronchial complaint and took frequent and copious draughts of an amber-coloured cough mixture, a remedy imported from his native land, and at times his legs were afflicted by a form of palsy, presumably the result of wounds sustained on the high veldt.

When Dad took me to meet Stewart in the workshop at the back of his shop the Scot was taking a dose of his cough mixture and on seeing me, and being appraised of the reason for my visit, he greeted me with a guttural Scottish expression of friendship: 'Aarrgh!' He led the way to the practice ground, carrying a hickory shaft which he occasionally used as a cane when his war wound troubled him. The old cut-down cleek with which I had been furnished felt impossibly heavy and clumsy in my youthful hands and naturally I gripped it with all my might in preparation to hit my first golf shot.

Crack! The lash of Stewart's cane brought tears to my eyes and broke the skin of my knuckles but my involuntary cry of pain was drowned by Stewart's shout of encouragement: 'Gleekit lummox!' The words meant nothing to me, but the warmth of their delivery endeared this rough diamond of a man to me and, of course, that first lesson was invaluable. Years later, when poised to win the Grand Slam, I found my hands tightening on the club and at that moment I felt again the admonitory tap of Stewart's cane and relaxed my grip.

Thanks to Stewart's perspicacity, I thus began my golf career with the priceless gift of a tension-free grip of the club. Other good golfing habits were imparted by Stewart with his usual economy of words. For some reason, possibly through youthful imitation of one of the club's better players, I took to tilting my head at the address until Stewart corrected this fault with a stinging clip around the ear from his massive right hand.

I bore the welts and bruises of my friend's continuing tuition with pride and fortitude, appreciative of his consideration in making absolutely sure that my swing should develop along the correct lines. I followed him everywhere like a faithful dog and saw through his patently feigned impatience at my presence, becoming extremely adept at leaping high in the air to avoid the playful swish of his cane. One matter perturbed me about our relationship. Stewart's cough, a curious wheezing groan from the back of the throat, seemed worse whenever I was around, requiring liberal doses of his special mixture. I was deeply moved by the response of this undemonstrative man when finally, having absorbed his wisdom and skilled tuition, I told him that the time had come when I must leave to make my way in the world of golf. He was seized by a coughing fit of such severity that it doubled him up, his red bandana stuffed into his mouth in a considerate attempt to keep the germs from me. When eventually this paroxysm subsided and he stood erect his blue eyes were suffused with tears.

When I won the national amateur championship at Merion in 1924, my first national success, I could hardly wait to get back to the Atlanta Athletic club to see Stewart and thank him for his unstinted help. I felt as a dog must feel, taking a thrown stick to lay at the feet of my master. Stewart was outwardly as aloof as ever but I was not fooled by his stony exterior. Inside, I knew well, he was seething with pride and excitement and eager to hear every detail of my adventure. He sat at his work bench, his head cupped in his hand like Rodin's sculpture 'Le Penseur' so that he could give his full concentration to my shot by shot account of those eight rounds. Astonishingly, I was able to remember every club, also the length of every putt and the subtleties of the breaks, and he was so absorbed that he uttered no word during my recital, his regular nasal breathing sounding for all the world like the purring of a contented cat.

It was quite late by the time I had completed my story but I could not refrain from imposing on my friend's limitless well of goodwill. I picked up a club and assumed the address position, seeking his professional opinion of what had caused me to hook the ball on occasion. Stewart shook himself from his pose of contemplation and rose to his feet, slightly unsteadily from his suppressed emotion. At the time I thought that his leg wound caused him slightly to lose his balance as he made a gesture resembling a pugilistic blow. His fist landed flush on my right shoulder causing me to spin round. Of course! I had been setting up to the ball with an open-shouldered stance. Trust my faithful mentor to put his finger on the trouble so acutely. No word passed between us as I left, rubbing my shoulder. Words are not necessary in a relationship as close as ours. The familiar plop of a cork being urgently drawn from a bottle was the last I heard of Stewart as I drove off.

11
Hogan Finds His Niche

Moot points are unsatisfactory. Nobody likes them because you don't know where you stand with a moot point. The only useful function historians perform is to settle moot points by researching all the evidence and coming down hard one way or another, as in decreeing that Adolf Hitler was a Bad Thing, or that the Virgin Queen really was, although she probably wouldn't have been if there had been quiet motels at the time of Sir Walter Raleigh.

Therefore golf's mootest point must be addressed: was Ben Hogan the last of the old era or the first of the modern era? Some people suggest that he was both, that, indeed, he invented the modern era. By the code of the historian such a proposition is absurd, almost cheating, since it leaves the point as moot as ever.

Let us review the evidence. He started to play with hickory clubs; he did not give interviews, fly his own plane, or consult sports psychologists. He wore clothing of sombre autumnal tints and on occasion was downright rude to Sam Snead. There is no recorded instance of his ever having made a joke, let alone a naughty one. So far, everything points directly to the old era. However, the conflict arises from some disturbing anachronisms. His greatest triumphs were achieved with modern equipment. He wore a rather racy white cap. He was a practice fiend and boringly absorbed by theory. Indeed, after years of agonized analysis he reinvented the golf swing by doing something obscure but immensely significant with the pressure of the fingers, or some of them, of the left-hand grip. All these characteristics are clearly modern and so the question remains delicately balanced.

However, there is a clincher which puts Hogan unquestionably into the modern era: he pioneered the use of the word 'pronate'. By so doing he threw golf instruction into total confusion, another modern practice. Some golfers in desperate search of enlightenment actually looked up pronate in the dictionary and only compounded their confusion. 'Pronate the wrists!' decreed Hogan. By this time Hogan's reputation for rebuffing supplicants was so rigidly established that nobody had the nerve to point out that when a golfer pronated one wrist he must perforce supinate the other. Which wrist, Mr Hogan? The question went unasked.

Fortunately, the action of pronating, or possibly supinating, is immaterial to the discussion. What matters is that Hogan used a word of such power that it totally obscured what he was saying. That is a technique which secures his place in the modern era, an innovation which has revolutionized the American way of life. Madison Avenue switched over exclusively to the use of words instead of ideas. Politicians were quick to see the possibilities of substituting words for policies, but the greatest beneficiary has been the catering business. It is a lengthy and skilful business to prepare delicious meals but by means of the Pronate Syndrome it is no longer necessary. All you have to do is conjure up some promising adjectives: 'Luscious, tenderized, Jumbo Chesapeake Bay prawns in exquisite piquant savoury sauce hinting at exotic oriental delicacies to titillate the palate of the most fastidious gourmet'. The dish is in fact tasteless, having been deep frozen in a cardboard pack ever since it left the factory a year previously. No matter. Because the restaurant is kept in Stygian gloom and his senses are further anaesthetized with an amplified rock band, the diner cannot tell the difference and is content with the savour of those delicious adjectives.

So it is with Hogan. Even the title of his book, *The Modern Fundamentals of Golf*, has scholars disputing like theologians over whether Modern Fundamentals means a whole new set of natural laws, replacing those tedious rules enunciated by Isaac Newton or, possibly, a modern interpretation of age-old fundamentals. As for the contents of this golfing Bible, the doctrine of the Immaculate Conception is child's play compared to Hogan's dissertation on the function of the left thumb.

Be that as it may, his achievements on the golf course were not obscured by verbiage. They shine from the record books with perfect clarity, none more brightly than his last US Open victory when, hovering between life and death after a horrendous car smash, he dragged his broken body from the hospital bed and beat the world. With his legs heavily bandaged Hogan inched his way painfully around Merion with the help of a walking frame, pausing from time to time to rifle one-iron shots at the flag.

When the winning putt dropped his adoring fans invaded the green in an unseemly scramble to steal that one iron. With its loss this very private man perforce had to retire into very private life, in open defiance of the Lone Star code that Texans must commit their lives to telling extravagant lies to anyone who will listen. Hogan never goes on television to brag about his greatness, which is old fashioned of him, but on balance he must be labelled as the first of modern era.

That leaves history with a delicate problem. How is Arnold Palmer to be designated? Somehow the title of The Best Golfing ex-Coastguard fails to define his place in the firmament of the game. Likewise, The Second of the Modern Era does him less than justice. There is nothing else for it: he will have to be subjected to a detailed scrutiny.

12
Adoration of the Arnold

Deacon switched on the wipers. The snow which had been falling in intermittent flakes like the drifting ash from a bonfire grew more intense. The last of the daylight was failing fast. Deacon was lost on a side road in Pennsylvania, and now the falling snow reflected the light from his headlamps back into his eyes and he could not read the road signs, if indeed there were any out in the backwoods. The needle on the gas gauge, he noted with concern, was nudging into the red warning zone.

At his side Doris gave a short, instantly suppressed, cry of pain. 'What is it, dear?' he asked. She looked at him with an expression of part fear, part apology: 'I think it's started.' 'Don't worry,' said Deacon, 'we'll find a place soon.' He pushed the Model T forward as fast as the visibility and road conditions warranted, pausing momentarily when the road forked. To the left Deacon saw a light in the sky, a greenish glow refracted by the snow flakes. He turned left and followed the light, resolutely ignoring turnings onto what looked like main highways. The blare of the Holiday Inn sign was upon him almost before he knew it and he skidded the Ford into the car park.

'You wait here while I fix up a room,' said Deacon. At the reception desk a bored clerk was lounging in her chair with her arms raised like a praying mantis, fingers at full stretch.

'Do you have a double room?'

The receptionist waved her nail lacquer brush in a languid gesture towards a sign on the counter reading 'No vacancies'.

'But my wife is going to have a baby. The contractions have already started.'

'Howard Johnson's down the road apiece. You could try there.'

Deacon's face hardened. 'We can't go any further, don't you understand? We must have a place here and now.'

The tone of his voice penetrated the cocoon of the girl's indifference. 'Well, there's a shack out back where they used to keep the beasts. It's clean and dry. You could maybe camp there.'

'Any chance of getting a doctor out here?' asked Deacon. The girl glanced out of the window. 'It's a real blizzard now. Nothing could move on these roads before they get the ploughs on them in the morning.'

Deacon unloaded his sleeping bag from the Ford and settled Doris in the shack. He broke up some empty fruit boxes and made a fire. The baby was born by the light of the flickering flames and Deacon swaddled it in one of his shirts. He laid it in Doris's arms. 'It's a boy!'

At that moment there was a commotion outside and three men entered. They looked disreputable to Deacon's suspicious eye, salesmen or maybe gamblers, but they seemed affable enough.

'I'd like to kick that sassy broad in the ass,' said one, adding quickly as his vision adjusted to the dim light and saw Doris: 'Begging your pardon, ma'am.'

'Wiseguys,' muttered Deacon to himself.

The strangers became warmly solicitous when they learned how Deacon had delivered his wife's baby in such surroundings.

'Gee,' said the one they called Dutch, 'I wish I had something to give the little feller, a birthday present of some kind. But we're flatter than a bust tyre.'

'Wait a minute,' said the short and swarthy one. 'We do have something we can give him.'

'What's that, Gene?'

'We can give him a blessing.' He drew a pencil from his pocket and gently folded the baby's fingers around it. 'This is how you hold the club.'

The man called Lighthorse approached the makeshift crib and bent low to whisper in the babe's ear: 'My gift if this – hit the living hell out of the ball.'

Dutch knelt by the crib and placed a hand lightly on the baby's head. 'My gift, little one, is to take something from you. By this laying on of hands I hereby remove the curse of mankind, the fear of a six-foot side-hiller.'

'. . . This is how you hold the club.'

The sun rose strongly and the roads were clear. The three men prepared to continue their journey. 'Tell me,' said Deacon. 'What do you do? You know, for a living.'

'We're golfers,' said Gene.

'Golf? They play that back in the old country,' said Deacon.

'And in the new country,' said Dutch.

When they had gone, Deacon went out to his car and found a full can of gas on the running board. 'Those golfers!' he said. 'They're not a bad bunch of guys.' He loaded Doris and the baby into the back of the Ford and drove away.

Down the road he saw a sign. 'Men wanted. Labourers required for the construction of Latrobe golf course.' He turned into the site. 'Maybe it's our lucky day, Doris. I might get work here. It's pretty country, might be a good place to settle. By the way, what are we going to call the kid?'

Doris smiled. 'What about Arnold?'

Deacon rolled the name around his tongue. 'Arnold. Arnold Palmer. It's got a kind of ring to it.'

The low morning sun shining through the blond fuzz of the baby's hair framed his face in a golden radiance.

13
Leave Nothing to Chance

'Have you seen my tartan bonnet anywhere?'
'Last time I saw it Jimmy was using it to polish his Cortina. Why do you need it, anyway? Going to a fancy-dress party?'

'No, local colour. There's a VIP arriving at the lodge this afternoon and I've got to babysit him. You know the drill, catch a fish for him so he can have it stuffed for his rumpus room.'

'Rich?'

'Stinking.'

'Big tipper?'

'You know those Yanks.'

'I've just remembered where the bonnet is. Sally's been using it as an oven glove. Still, I wish you didn't have to stoop to these cheap theatricals just to impress the punters at the lodge. That bonnet makes you look a right prat.'

'Don't be silly, Doris, it's just business.'

Douglas painted his chin with spirit gum and carefully applied a lurid ginger beard. 'How do I look? Ethnic enough?'

'Like I said, you look a proper prat. Here's your bonnet.'

Douglas took a box of lead shot and poured the contents into the rubber-lined poacher's pocket of his heavy tweed jacket.

'What on earth is that for?'

Douglas winked. 'Trick of the trade. Slip lead shot into the gills and the fish weighs heavier. And you know the rule: the heavier the fish, the heavier the tip. See you later.'

He picked up his thumb-stick and made his way towards the lodge, humming the 'Skye Boat Song' as he went to put himself in a properly highland frame of mind.

The lodge manager was fawning unashamedly in front of the visitor. 'Ah, here's the man of the moment. Meet Dougal, the finest gillie on the Spey. If Dougal can't find you a fish then there aren't any fish to be found. Isn't that right, Dougal?'

Douglas took the visitor's hand and, as always on these occasions, suffered a momentary panic that he might fluff his lines. He cleared his throat and launched into his spiel: 'Heich o' fash I am tae mak your a-cquain-tance, sair, gleekit lummox dun whinny east neuk siller tassie broomy law kittle kink, ye ken, whaup's neuk, canty lye drum sichty the noo, braw fush reet fine hinny moon the nicht.'

'Cut the whimsical tourist crap,' said the visitor, 'I'm here to fish.'

'Oh, very well, sir,' said Douglas.

'Meet me here seven o'clock sharp in the morning. And one more thing.'

'Sir?'

'Lose that dumb beard.'

'Very good, sir.'

Doris took the TV dinner from the microwave oven and passed it to Douglas. 'How did it go? What's your punter like?'

Douglas winced as he tugged at the ginger beard. 'You were quite right. He took one look at me and had me sussed as a prat.'

'What is the pH value?' The brisk authority of the angler's question caught Douglas off guard.

'The what was that, sir?'

'Never mind. I'll measure it myself.' The angler waded into the Spey until the water was nearly up to the top of his thigh boots. From his back-pack he took a test tube, dipped it into the water and busied himself with litmus sticks, comparing the results against a colour chart and noting the readings in a pocket book.

Next he drew out a thermometer and took several readings, in the shallows, in the deep pools along the bank and in the main current. Again he wrote down the results.

Out came a light meter which he held up to the sky, pointing it first

'. . . and drew back the rod with a pronounced tilting of the shoulders.'

at a dark cloud and then at a brighter patch where the sun was making a vain attempt to break through the overcast. He made some more notes.

He took a small anemometer and a compass from the pack and measured the wind strength and direction, noting the details in his book. Finally he dipped a finger into the water and tested it on his tongue before wading ashore.

'The mountain snow is melting early this year. By the seasonal norm the spate isn't due for another ten days. And another thing. There's a distillery upstream.'

'You know these parts then, sir?'

'Never been here before in my life. What about that distillery?'

'You're right, there is. The Glen Hoddle distillery is about two miles upstream.'

'Single malt, right? Ring the manager and find out if he proposes to sluice his mash bins again this week. That's all we can do here today. Pack up the tackle.'

'Are we not going to try for a fish, sir?'

The angler fixed Douglas with a laser stare: 'Of course not. We're going to the tennis courts.'

He led the way back to the lodge at a brisk pace and laid his handkerchief flat in the centre of the court.

'Assemble the rod.'

While Douglas slotted the lengths of split cane together and attached the reel, the angler produced an apothecary's balance from his pack and carefully weighed a selection of salmon flies, the Silver Doctor, Jack Scott and the Durham Ranger. For the next seven hours the angler practised casting while Douglas scuttled to and fro returning the handkerchief to its spot after each successful strike.

Not until the angler had satisfied himself that he could drop his fly on the handkerchief from any point of the compass, upwind, crosswind and downwind, did he finally order Douglas to pack up the rod. It was dusk.

'I won't be needing you tomorrow. Work to do.'

Douglas slumped into his armchair in front of the television set. For once Sir Robin Day's eye slits lacked their mesmerizing power. Douglas was immune through sheer exhaustion.

'You make this chap sound like a proper ogre,' said Doris.

'Monster or genius – what's the difference?'

'But would you judge him to be a generous man?'

'From the way he carries on, I'd guess that he has a sliding scale for tips, ten cents an ounce or something like that.'

In this surmise Douglas was later to be proved quite wrong, to his delight and not without a pang of guilt. He slept late, stirring fitfully at dawn when a helicopter clattered overhead on its way to the lodge.

It set down on the tennis court and the angler climbed aboard. 'Edinburgh University,' he ordered, 'department of entomology.'

That evening Dr Mark Wilson, Carnegie Professor of Natural History and internationally renowned author of *Nymphs and Pupae of Speyside*, staggered into the fellows' common room gasping: 'A dram! A dram! No, make that a double. I feel as if I have been grilled by the Spanish Inquisition on the life cycle of every flying insect known to science. How the hell would I know if *Salmo samar* can detect the pheromones of the genus *Ephemeris* through water?'

The following day the angler returned to the river bank with Douglas bent under the weight of theodolite, measuring rods, range-finder, sonar and hydrostatic equipment. Ten hours later the map was finished. No quarter-mile stretch of river could ever before have been so meticulously plotted. Every rock in the river bed was accurately tabulated, the currents and eddies calculated to two decimal points of depth and flow, the temperatures logged and the chemical analysis of the water noted.

The manager of the lodge greeted the returning angler: 'I managed to get a telex machine sent up from Perth as you requested. Here is the full forecast from the meteorological office.'

He handed the angler a two-yard scroll of closely printed details about isobars, jet stream and occluded fronts. The angler studied it closely and then turned to Douglas: 'Right. Six o'clock on the tennis court for warm-up casting. River at 11.15.'

'We're going to try for a fish, sir?'

'Correction. We are not going to try anything. I am going to catch a fish.'

Next morning Douglas greeted the angler: 'It's a grand day for fishing, sir. Not too bright although I fancy we might see the sun later.'

'Not at 11.15 we won't,' snapped the angler.

'Maybe you're right,' said Douglas, 'and there's not too much wind to break up the water.'

'Of course there isn't. I made sure of that.'

The practice casting session went well and the angler marched confidently down to the river. He seemed to have withdrawn into himself, oblivious of everything around him and glowing with an inner intensity. He consulted his notebook and scanned the river. 'Give me the Wilkinson.' He deftly attached the fly and, looking neither to the right nor the left, strode into the water. He stopped at the point he had determined for his cast, shuffling his feet among the pebbles to ensure a firm footing.

He squinted at the water, cocked his head slightly to the right and drew back the rod with a pronounced tilting of the shoulders. A flick of his powerful wrists despatched the fly unerringly to his chosen target. Instantly the rod bowed and the reel screeched on the strike as the line was drawn out by the speeding fish.

The angler pronated his right wrist, bringing the line on top of the rod which he transferred to his left hand. He rested his right hand on the spinning reel, applying slight pressure to arrest the salmon's run.

It was a strong fish. By the lore of the river it is customary to describe fighting fish as game or brave, although common sense tells us that desperation rather than courage makes the sport. At such times anglers become so engrossed in playing the fish that the passage of time loses all meaning and on this occasion Douglas's testimony is not to be trusted. In the following months when telling the story in the public bar of the Dog with Two Cocks the time varied from four to seven hours, according to the lateness of the hour.

Suffice to say, the angler eventually signalled for the net. The angler slid the net under the exhausted fish and waded ashore with his prize. Douglas was exhilarated.

'My, sir, but you're a wonder. That's a bonny fish, twenty pounds if it's an ounce.'

'What's the record rod-and-line catch on the Spey?'

'You've got me there,' said Douglas. 'That would be something exceptional, no doubt, fifty pounds or more. Your fish, grand enough though it is and right proud you can be of it, would hardly be classified as a specimen fish but it is a right beauty for all that.'

'Not even a specimen fish?'

The angler gently released the hook from the salmon's jaw and contemptuously released the fish into the river.

'Jack Nicklaus is interested only in majors.'

14
The Boy in the Bush

No, it was not a tigress. And Gary Player was never suckled by a wild beast. Yet that foolish legend was not all that far off the mark for he was deeply influenced by the environment of the high veldt and the law of the jungle. As a young boy, barely out of the toddler stage, he was for ever giving his nurse the slip and running off alone into the bush. There he learned the basic rules of life through communion with the animals. This, it should be stressed right from the start, is not one of those sentimental stories about a juvenile Dr Doolittle who could talk with the animals in their own languages. Animals cannot talk, as we all understand very well. We are also aware, however, that communication is possible between man and beast. By his sullen demeanour and doleful, even accusing, glances, the dog tells its master that it is not thrilled by the new brand of dog biscuits. The man explains that the supermarket was out of the favourite Fido-Fare. By leaving three of the biscuits untouched and not even sniffed at, the dog conveys the message that this lapse demonstrated a woeful disregard for its well being and that it had better not happen again. Of course, replies the man, a consignment of Fido-Fare is expected any day and he will stockpile a huge reserve to meet any similar emergencies in the future.

That is really quite a complex exchange of ideas and information and it was achieved without words. True, the man uttered words, but since the dog did not understand them literally they were not truly words in the sense of messages. It was all done by nuance and gesture and tone of voice.

If a surburban chartered accountant can communicate with a basset hound at such a level it requires no great flight of imagination to understand how a child of many generations living among wild animals could get onto their wavelength and exchange observations on the nature and purpose of life. It would be immensely tedious to explain every detail of how they conversed because every species has its own body language with extensive vocabularies of signs for fear, suspicion, welcome, agreement, contentment, etc. So for purposes of brevity and clarity the exchanges between boy and beast will be transposed into the common idiom of human conversation.

The other question which sceptics will surely raise is how a defenceless boy could survive amongst hungry predators. Partly this was due to the maternal instinct, that powerful force which protects infants of all species like a guardian angel and which nourished Romulus and Remus among a pack of ravening wolves.

There was also the matter of the boy's size. He was small and scrawny with not enough meat on him to make a decent meal, even with extra bread and a side order of baked potato. Frankly, there wasn't enough nourishment on him to warrant the labour of picking tiny tit-bits from the carcase. Lots of people feel that way about shrimps, on the grounds that the expenditure of energy for so little reward will result in a nett calorie loss, leaving them hungrier than when the meal started. Such considerations are important in the jungle.

The first animal to fill the boy's eyes with wonder and delight was the springbok. While the sentinel adults kept watch for carnivores the younger members of the herd dashed around a clearing, leaping improbable heights every few paces. The boy approached a mature male: 'Tell me, why do they keep jumping like that? They're not jumping *over* anything, just jumping.'

'You must understand,' said the springbok, 'that we are a species of committed Darwinians. Most animals are, as you will discover. We believe in the survival of the fittest. Those youngsters are engaged in callisthenics to make them agile, strong and swift. One day that ability to jump as if from a trampoline will save their lives. A springing lioness with outstretched claw can reach up about six feet into the air. So the springbok has to be able to take off at a split second's notice and clear seven feet. Understand?'

'Makes sense to me,' said the boy. 'Should I learn to jump seven feet?'

70

'You are not a springbok. Your natural defence against the lion, as you will learn in time, is a Magnum 400. But you would do well to absorb the principle that it is not enough to be fit; you have to be the fittest in order to survive.'

Even so the boy tried a few speculative jumps as he ran home. That evening he sent off for a Charles Atlas course in body building. On his next excursion the boy was studying a bull elephant when the beast asked, 'Why are you looking at me like that?'

'To be honest, I was thinking that you did not look exceptionally fit. Flabby and ponderous, I'd say.'

'Oh, I'm fit enough,' said the elephant, breaking off a heavy branch with its trunk to make the point, 'but fitness in the evolutionary context is not confined to muscle tone. Intellectual horse power can be just as important as brute strength.'

'Are you an intellectual then?'

'Not in the sense that they use the term in the wine bars around Broadcasting House or the hall of All Souls' College. But we have prodigious memories and the accumulation of remembered experiences down the aeons does constitute a kind of wisdom. My advice to you, young feller, is to store everything away in your memory. Obscure rules of golf, old grudges, the way different varieties of sand affect the dynamics of the ball, how many miles you fly in a year, faces, names, smutty jokes, yardages of championship courses, indeed any old dross. Never know when it might come in handy.'

'How did you know I was interested in golf?'

'Easy. Many years ago Bobby Locke tried to shoot me. He missed because the shot pulled left but I never forgot that he had a white left hand. Sure sign of a golfer, just like yours. So, never forget. And one more thing: beware of dentists.'

The boy ran home and wrote away for a course in Pelmanism. The next day he was walking along a jungle track when a cobra reared up, extending its hood and hissing viciously.

'I can understand why you reach up and bare your fangs,' said the boy, 'but the hiss bothers me. You are all set to strike at your prey but the hiss is surely counter-productive because it gives advance warning to your victim.'

The cobra sank back into a comfortable coil. 'It saves venom. You have

71

no idea of the effort it takes to top up your supply of venom. Your glands ache for days. I wasn't out to kill you, just stop you from stepping on me. Of course I had to be ready with the lethal injection just in case, but we succeed as a species mainly by hissing.'

'Would hissing work for me?'

'Not hissing. But talking should do just as well. The principle is the same. I daresay that you humans could vocalize fear, or boredom, or any other response to each other. The trick is the hint of menace in the background.'

The boy could hardly wait to experiment with the idea of speech as a weapon in the battle of survival. Back at home he went to the stable and experimented on the family donkey. Next morning at breakfast the boy's father was perplexed. 'Darndest thing,' he said, 'the donkey was as right as rain yesterday, but today it's got no hind legs!'

In the weeks that followed the boy conversed with every animal he could find and learnt many valuable lessons. The rhino taught him when to charge and the hippo impressed on him the importance of regular bowel movements. The bushbok expounded the advantages of the lone individual over the herd system. He was fascinated by the swooping fish eagle and remarked that the bird was lucky to have inherited the talent to strike so surely every time.

'Luck has nothing to do with it,' snapped the eagle. 'Every fish I take represents thousands of practice dives on bits of driftwood. The more I practise the luckier I get.'

The lesson which was to prove of the greatest value to the boy was provided by the cheetah. He congratulated the sleek cat on its exceptional turn of speed and remarked that this must be the secret of the species' survival.

'Of course it is useful to us to be nippy on our feet, but that's not the secret. After all, we could just stretch out on a branch and drop on any animal which passed below, the way the big snakes do. No, our forte is old-fashioned persistence. Once I get my teeth into a throat you could not lever my jaws open with a crowbar. I get rolled on and squashed against tree trunks and ripped by hooves and horns and claws but, no matter how much it hurts, I hang on. Sooner or later I drag down even the biggest and toughest of them.'

Gary Player practised until his fingers bled, although he never

'. . . the boy conversed with every animal he could find . . .'

reached the level of skill of the fish eagle. But thanks to the animals he tore out everybody's throat and became the King of the Jungle.

15
Dark Powers

Stubby Laidlaw, Captain US Marine Corps, commander of Baker company, studied the summary of evidence with conflicting emotions. As a golfer he had a certain sympathy with the sergeant of his machine-gun section. As a professional soldier he was appalled by what he read. He mused on the colonel's words: 'I leave it to your judgement whether it's a full-blown court-martial or something more imaginative. Just so long as the Corps comes out clean and there is not the slightest possibility that the general ever sets eyes on that horse's ass again.'

Captain Laidlaw sighed deeply and instructed the provost sergeant to bring in the miscreant. Sergeant Trevino marched into the company office and saluted.

'At ease, Lee,' said Captain Laidlaw wearily. 'You've really got my ass in a sling this time. And your own. Is it true that you called the general a lousy piker and a two-star sonofabitch?'

'I did.'

'But why?'

'Because I couldn't think of anything worse on the spur of the moment. If I could do it over I'd call him a pot-bellied flake and a two-timing skunk as well.'

'Careful, Trevino. This is a serious charge. We could be talking two years in the stockade and a dishonourable discharge.'

'For me or him?' replied Trevino truculently. 'He's the one who should be dishonourably discharged.'

'I gather you claim extreme provocation in your defence, something about an unpaid bet.'

'It's called welshing. That four-flushing polecat. . . .'

'That'll do, Sergeant. Now, let's see. You were detailed to play golf with General Heffelfinger and reported to the first tee. You offered the General six strokes a side. What's his handicap?'

'He said he was a ten. I was being generous.'

'And then you suggested a little interest in the game to spice up the action. Tell me about your proposal.'

'Well, sir, I offered a five buck Nassau, automatic presses, a six pack for greenies and a free crack at his WAAC driver if I made a hole in one.'

'Did the General agree to these terms?'

'He just said, "Hit the ball, Sergeant." Back at Tennison Park that means the bets are down. No argument, no objection.'

'And how did the match come out?'

'I took him three ways. That's fifteen bucks, right. Six presses brings it up to forty-five, plus a gallon and a half of Budweiser. I missed out on that top-heavy blonde by this much at the 16th.'

'What happened at the end of the game?'

'Well, I stood there rubbing my hands and grinning expectantly and he just said, "Thanks for the game, Sergeant." So I said something about a game not being over until the formalities had been completed. He just walked over to his car and that's when the extreme provocation hit me.'

'I see. Obviously there was a misunderstanding. They do things differently at West Point than Tennison Park.'

'I never was at West Point, Captain.'

'No. I can see how you might have assumed that a wager had been struck.'

'Right. A debt of honour.'

'Even so, Trevino, you committed a gross act of insubordination. I ought to bust your ass, but in view of the special circumstances I think we can handle this through regular military channels. As a serving marine you are liable to posting anywhere in the world at a moment's notice, right?'

'Yessir. Of course.'

'You couldn't call a posting punishment.'

'I guess not.'

'All in the line of duty.'

'That's right, sir.'

'You could never consider yourself to be the victim of injustice if you were suddenly ordered to new duty.'

'No, sir.'

'Well, as it happens, an experienced sergeant is urgently needed for an important assignment. You're it, Trevino. Get your gear together and your orders will be cut this afternoon. You fly out this evening.'

'Where am I going, Captain?'

'Oh, didn't I mention it? You're the new guard sergeant at the American embassy in Haiti. There is no golf course on Haiti as far as I know. Travel in civilian clothes, that's the rule on these diplomatic postings.'

Sergeant Trevino sat in the embassy guard room at Port au Prince. It was like a sauna. It was also boring. Levenworth could not have been worse than this, reflected Trevino. He picked up the daily duty roster and lashed at the flies which tormented him without cease. It was as if the entire fly population of this Godforsaken island had sworn a vendetta against him. Why couldn't they pester somebody else for a change? Why not go and torment Baboo, the civilian clerk. Clerk! One of Papa Doc's Tonton Macoute and everyone knew it. Come to think of it, Trevino could not recall ever having seen Baboo flap at a fly. He studied Baboo intently. There's no flies on Baboo, he mused. What the hell did that expression mean? How did it start? At that moment a large blue-bottle made a standard turn to starboard and droned towards the clerk. Baboo opened one eye and glanced at the approaching fly, which promptly dropped like a stone to the floor. Heart attack? Wing tissue fatigue? Trevino intensified his vigil. It happened again. And again. When the fourth fly bit the dust at Baboo's feet Trevino snapped: 'How did you do that?'

'What's that, boss?'

'You know damn well what. You killed that fly without touching it.'

'This is Haiti, boss. Strange things happen.'

'So I've heard. But you made that happen. How do you do it?'

'It's the power, boss. You have to have the power.'

'Can you give me the power? Teach me how to get the power.'

Baboo pondered this request. 'Cost plenty to learn the power, boss.'

'Like how much?'

'Five dollars, American. And plenty beer from the PX.'

'Damn! The power might just work on a golf ball.'

'You've got it,' said Trevino. 'When do I start?'

'Midnight tonight, boss. Come to the deserted shack down by the mangrove swamp. Bring a six-pack. Also a live chicken.'

Sergeant Trevino's hitch was over. On the bus to El Paso he reflected that military service had probably been a mistake. Golf was his life and always had been. Even if he couldn't make it on the Tour the world was full of pigeons. He and Claudia could always live on pigeon pie.

In the event, as the record books show, he did much better the second time around as a pro golfer. For instance, he did well enough to tie Jack Nicklaus for the US Open at Merion. That meant a play-off. Trevino was confident. He liked head to head golf, or eyeball to eyeball as he preferred to call it. He put a plastic snake in his golf bag. That would make a great gag to relieve the tension on the first tee. It would help his image as the irrepressible joker, the good old boy who wouldn't hurt a fly.

Four times during the round he managed to catch Nicklaus's eye at a critical moment. That was enough. He won by four shots. Nicklaus made no excuses for his defeat. That was not his style. But later he entered John Hopkins' Hospital for exhaustive tests to discover the reason for sudden muscle spasms. The doctors could find nothing wrong with him.

The next year in the British Open at Muirfield Trevino experimented with inanimate objects. In the bathroom at his hotel he caused a tooth glass to jump off the shelf and shatter on the floor. Damn! The power might just work on a golf ball.

He sank an outrageous pitch and holed two trap shots. He was careful not to overdo it. Hell, he could play well enough to hold his own without using the power. Just a nudge now and then to guarantee keeping in contention. He laughed off his wonder shots. 'God is a Mexican,' he quipped.

In the final round he played the 17th hole like a hacker. He drove into a pot bunker, chopped out and hooked the next one to Hades. All he could do was take a big slash and hope. The ball finished behind the green in a hopeless position on a downslope in a sandy lie. He appraised the situation objectively. Tony Jacklin was a racing certainty for the title, barring miracles. So be it. A few miracles were needed.

Lee gave a perfunctory swing with his wedge and locked his gaze onto the ball, directing it unerringly into the hole. He looked across the green at Jacklin. Their eyes met. Jacklin lost all feeling in his hands. The shaft of his putter turned into a venomous snake. In the circumstances his next three putts were triumphs of willpower and iron self-control. Trevino strolled to victory.

On reflection he realized that his performance at Muirfield had been clumsy and absurdly obvious. He would have to be more subtle in future. Instead of that flashy guiding of his ball into the hole it would be just as easy to nudge his opponent's ball half an inch wide of the cup.

That Jacklin seemed particularly susceptible to manipulation, he reflected when they ran up against each other in the world match-play championship. Their match was a classic, a real ding dong. The huge crowd went wild. Trevino contrived a great show for them, taking the match into extra holes. Eventually he became bored. Besides, he was getting peckish; he always liked to eat early. Nobody noticed when his long putt changed course by a degree or two to roll directly into the middle of the hole. True, Jacklin shook his head in disbelief, but he did not know what he was disbelieving. He was never quite the same player again. That evening he had a chat with Nicklaus. They agreed that Trevino was something else.

16
The Price of Fame

'Tell me, Vicente. You know when you wrap that string round a golf club?'

'So.'

'Well, how do you make it without tying a knot and so that both ends of the string are tucked up under the coils? It's a miracle.'

'You donkey-head, Manolo,' said Baldomero. 'It's obvious. You tuck the ends under the coils with a knife.'

'No you don't,' said Vicente. 'And it's not a miracle. It's just a sort of trick. Both of you come to the club and I'll show you. And if you're polite to the caddymaster you might get to carry the bag of one of the nobles.'

'Can I come too, please, Vicente?' piped up baby Seve.

'Don't be silly, *muchacho*. You're far too young to go to the club. Eat up your *desayuno* and go out to play.'

'*Cerdo!*' said Seve. 'Golf! Golf! Golf! That's all you guys talk about. I wouldn't go to your stinking old club if you paid me a million *pesetas*. I'm off to the beach.'

The barefoot boy ran quickly from the farmhouse so that his brothers would not see the tears of his disappointment. How could Vicente say he was too young? Hell, he was *cuatro*, practically a man. He'd show them one day.

Seve made his way to the shore. The beach was deserted, as usual in mid-winter. He removed a couple of rocks from the pile alongside the breakwater and drew from his secret hiding place the stick he had whittled with his teeth. He reached into the recess and pulled out the piece of rusty angle iron he had salvaged from the town rubbish tip. Deftly he attached

81

the angle iron to the end of his stick by binding it with wire. He made two languid practice swings with the makeshift club and then dragged a pebble towards him onto a smooth area of sand.

He took great care setting himself to the pebble, making small adjustments to the set of his shoulders and hip so that they were exactly square to the line of his shot. His target was six *metros* to the left of a crimson buoy bobbing on rollers about 200 *metros* out in the Bay of Biscay.

Crack! The pebble flew as if along a string and splashed into the sea six *metros* to the left of the buoy. Seve cursed, using the word his parents had forbidden him to use in the house. He dragged another pebble towards him and pondered the problem. He knew that he could hit the buoy with a straight shot, or with a high slice, or with a raking, low draw or a soaring hook. There *must* be a way of hitting a low fade. He had to master that shot. How could he call himself a golfer like his brothers if he could not hit a low fade?

Maybe the secret lay in an adjustment of his grip. He rejected that idea even as it formed in his mind. He had been down that road before. It had taken him months of trial and error before he had settled on the arrangement of the back of the left hand facing the target and left thumb on top of the stick, then with the right hand as a mirror image, with the palms opposed in the same plane, little finger resting lightly in the crevice formed by the first and second fingers of the left hand, the right thumb alongside rather than on top of the stick. Even when he settled on this formation as the most effective way of gripping the club there was still something missing. The discovery came by accident. After hitting pebbles for ten hours a day his hands became sore, blistered and bleeding so badly that he could not stand the pain of gripping the stick tightly. To his astonishment he found that the more lightly he held the stick the better he could control the club and the harder he could hit his pebbles. The salt spray soon healed his lesions. No, he would not change his grip; for better or worse he would remain faithful to his painfully acquired method of holding the stick.

Opening the face of the club was not enough by itself. The pebble faded right enough but it always flew high. Keeping the hands well in front of the pebble at impact, plus an open club-face, certainly produced a low fade but it was a feeble shot, 150 *metros* at most, and of very limited value. What about opening the stance and swinging from out to in along the line of the toes? Or hitting a regular shot but supinating the wrists through the impact

82

zone? Obviously Vicente knew how to hit a low fade; Vicente knew everything. But Seve would bite out his own tongue before he asked anyone for help. He had to do it alone, his way.

He laboured for four hours, hitting 300 or more pebbles, in his search for the key move which would keep the pebble low and curving from left to right in a controlled swerve. He was so engrossed in his quest that he did not notice the stranger who strolled up and squatted on the breakwater, a keenly interested spectator of the boy's exercise. Finally Seve turned away in disgust at one particularly unsuccessful shot and he saw the stranger. He was dressed entirely in black, a handsome fellow with a trim pointed beard and curling moustaches. The stranger raised his hat, revealing a head of curly black hair from which protruded two short horns.

'*Buenos dias.*'

'Who are you?'

'My friends call me Mephisto.'

'What do you want?'

'Want? Nothing at all. On the contrary I wish nothing more than to give you something. It is obvious that you are trying to unravel the mysteries of the low fade. Toughest shot in golf. Even Tommy Bolt had trouble with it and if he couldn't make a shot then nobody could. Except me. I could teach you.'

'How do I know that you can hit low fades?'

The stranger leaped nimbly down from the breakwater, grabbed the club and in a blur of reciprocating swings directed a machine gun burst of pebbles in a low, curving trajectory. The pebbles pinged against the buoy like the evening Angelus.

Seve was impressed. 'Slow it down a bit so I can see how you do it.'

'Certainly. But first let us agree on an amicable arrangement. I am a collector of souls. Let me have your soul and in exchange for that worthless trifle I shall reveal the secret of the low fade.'

'It's a deal,' said Seve. 'Take it. It's all yours, just as soon as you teach me the knack of that accursed shot.'

Mephisto whispered urgently into the boy's ear. 'You've got the sidespin right, but you're getting to the bottom of the ball and imparting too much backspin. That's why the pebble is flying so high. The trick is to take the pebble fractionally thin, not a half top or anything gross like that but just

What would an ignorant four-year-old boy know about souls?'

thin enough to reduce the r.p.m.s while still making a solid contact. Try it.'

Seve set himself to a pebble and swung the club. The pebble flew off low and fast like a frightened quail and then swerved gently to the right, knocking off a flake of red paint as it clattered against the buoy.

'Now for your side of the bargain,' said Mephisto, opening his carpet bag.

'Help yourself,' said Seve.

Mephisto stretched out his hand and clasped at the air. He frowned. 'Where is it?'

'Search me,' said Seve. 'What would an ignorant four-year-old boy know about souls? That's your department.'

Mephisto scrabbled desperately in the air, growing more agitated by the minute. 'Curses! You haven't got a soul! Never come across a case like this in all my millennia. I've been wasting my time.'

So saying, he disappeared in a puff of sulphurous smoke.

Seve resumed his practice. When it grew so dark that he could no longer see the buoy he dismantled his club and stowed away the component parts in their hiding place. As he walked home to the farm he reflected that it had been a useful session, thanks to the episode with Mephisto. Funny business, that, not unlike the time six months previously when he had acquired the finest short game in the history of golf.

What had that other stranger called himself? Curious name. Ah yes, that was it: Beelzebub.

17

The Man of Iron

A shadow fell across Greta's paperback Jeffrey Archer. She resisted the instinct to look up, remembering the training that had earned her the position of seniorclinicaccidentreceptionist. First rule of hospital administration: make the sick feel guilty for wasting the time of busy and highly qualified professionals.

Greta continued to stare at the book, but she was not reading. Five minutes was the recommended time for ignoring patients, although the international symposium at Prague that summer had reached a consensus, following a well-documented address by the consultant behavioural psychologist for the British Department of Social Services, that seven minutes was preferable. Field trials had demonstrated that after seven minutes of being ignored some 78 per cent of the general public disappeared, taking their tiresome problems with them.

Greta composed her face into the expression which proclaimed bored contempt and indifference for the miserable speciment of sub-humanity she was about to confront and glanced up, reinforcing the effect with the impatient tone of her interrogatory *'Ja?'*

The labourer shuffled in embarrassment and felt himself shrinking. When he tried to speak the only sound which ushered from his parched mouth was a falsetto squeak. He cleared his throat and tried again: 'It's my foot.'

Greta read the signs and went for the kill. 'Your *foot*?' As intended, the labourer felt as he had the day he had noisily broken wind while kneeling to receive the sacrament.

'Well,' he stammered, 'my toe actually.'

She eviscerated him with her next inflexion: 'Toe?'

By now the labourer was perspiring and flustered. He blabbered: 'The big toe. Ingrowing toenail. Did I mention it was the right foot, septic, pus, you know?'

Greta decided that some shred of dignity and self-esteem still lingered within the man's psyche. That would never do. There was nothing else for it, she would have to hit him with the full castration treatment.

'Are you telling me that you have come to hospital because of a *toenail*? Tell me, pray, what do you imagine chiropodists are for? . . .'

At that moment Dr Stein barged through the swing doors. 'Goodnight, Greta. Hello, what's this? Another patient? I was hoping to get away early.'

'It's nothing, Herr Doctor, just an infected toenail. I am referring it to a chiropodist.'

Dr Stein paused. 'Infection? Toenails can be tricky. I'd better take a look at it.' He turned and marched briskly back into the surgery.

'Well, don't keep the doctor waiting,' snapped Greta. 'In you go.'

Dr Stein peered at the inflamed toe. He prodded it with his finger and then bent over and sniffed it. He feigned a look of deep concern although truth to tell, labourers' feet being labourers' feet, it took no great effort on his part to convey dismay.

'Gangrene! Prep him, nurse. I must operate immediately. Go with the nurse and we'll soon take care of that toe.'

The labourer rose from the examination couch and bent to retrieve his boot. 'Don't bother with that,' said Dr Stein. 'I'm afraid we're going to have to amputate. At the hip.'

'I'm sorry to be such a nuisance,' said the labourer. 'Keeping you from your dinner, Herr Doctor.'

Dr Stein snapped off his gloves and tugged down his mask. 'Thank you, everyone. Good work. Wrap up that leg, will you, Sister, and have it put in my car. I'll take it back to my lab for dissection. I'm preparing a paper on gangrene for the college of physicians.'

Back at the Schloss Löwenbräu Dr Stein carried the precious bundle down the winding stone stairs to the cellar. He unlocked the door and snapped on the light, illuminating the gleaming coils of the 20 megawatt condenser, the rows of specimen jars and, most pertinently for this was his immediate destination, the operating table on which lay the mortal remains of a male adult. In truth it represented the partial remains of many adults, the sundry components neatly stitched together to form one composite being which lacked only a right leg.

This omission Dr Stein now proceeded to remedy. He checked that the head of the femur fitted snugly into the alien socket and then went to work with clamps and sutures, stitching quickly and surely. It was a routine task and Dr Stein allowed his mind to dwell on the next, and vital, phase of his experiment. The theory was sound enough, of that he was confident. All matter was comprised of atoms, neutrons in electrically stimulated orbit around a proton, and for atoms the concept of life and death did not apply. They were indestructible. So, therefore, the molecules which comprised matter, including human tissue, could equally be made immortal if only the process of degeneration could be arrested. The key, Dr Stein had concluded as a young student, must lie within the electrical fields of matter. If it was eternal in atoms there must be a way of reversing its mortality in cells. From that basic thesis Dr Stein had devoted a lifetime of research and experiment. His failures had been many, a long series of human limbs and organs broiled to medium rare, but at last he had refined his calculations and technique to the point where success was virtually assured.

He tied off the final stitch, neatly severed the thread with his teeth and stood back. All was ready. The laboratory shook with a faint tremor and small particles of whitewash floated like dandruff from the ceiling as the great clock chimed the hour.

'Damn that bell,' he muttered, more from habit than conviction. In fact he was inordinately proud of the great clock. Visitors came from all over Transylvania to stare at the famous sixteenth-century clock of Schloss Löwenbräu, and take photographs of this fine example of the mediaeval horologist's art. The bell itself was fashioned as the trunk of a mighty oak tree and the striker was a full-sized representation in cast iron of a woodman wielding an axe. On the hour the woodman swung out of an aperture in the bell tower and struck the tree with his axe.

At least Dr Stein would have a full hour without further interruption and that should be plenty of time to conclude the final dramatic act of restoring life to the unliving. He threw the main switch of the generator and gazed intensely at the compressor dials as the current built up towards the critical level. A jagged blue stream of electrical discharge flashed between the electrodes on either side of the subject on the operating table.

High in the cumulo-nimbus cloud above the Schloss Löwenbräu a similar reaction was beginning. The first arc of lightning illuminated the forest.

Dr Stein moved to the operating table and observed the subject closely. It would take a while. He passed the time by cutting back the ingrowing toenail, cleaning the lesion and giving the dead leg an injection of broad spectrum antibiotic.

'That's better!'

Dr Stein stepped back in astonishment. The subject's eyelids flickered. The eyes opened. The mouth moved: 'I feel like a goddamn rag doll.' He raised an arm and tentatively flexed the fingers.

'Keep still,' said Dr Stein, barely able to speak for excitement. 'You must rest until your transplants have healed. By the way, welcome back to the land of the living.'

Outside, the storm raged. The lightning, drawn to the highest conductor, struck repeatedly around the belfry. The spindle on which the woodman's turntable revolved snapped with a loud crack. The cast-iron figure toppled and fell. Accelerating at thirty-two feet per second per second, it crashed through the roof of Schloss Löwenbräu, regained impetus after this momentary obstacle, smashed through the floor below and continued to plummet through the bedroom floor, through the obersitzenplatz floor, and finally through the dining-room floor. The obverse side of this last obstruction was, of course, the laboratory ceiling. The iron woodman landed smack on top of the subject which by now was calling loudly for bratwurst and a stein of beer. It was squashed to pulp in an explosion of popping stitches.

Dr Stein fainted.

The generator continued to burn and the arc of electrical discharge threw a blue sheen over the rusting figure. Gradually the surface of the woodman took on a yellowish pallor which slowly turned to a russet glow. The figure sat up, looked around and climbed down from the operating table, brushing particles of charred flesh from his person.

He threw aside his axe and bent over the prostrate doctor. The first thing he needed was an identity. After that he would be able to fend for himself;

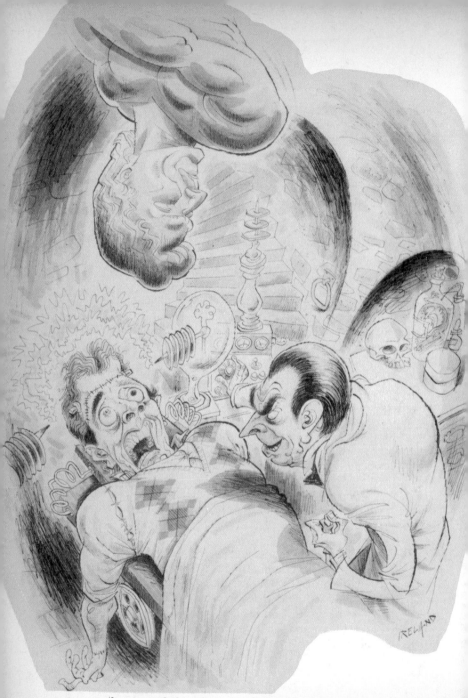

'It was squashed to pulp in an explosion of popping stitches.'

there must be some occupation in this human world which would be suited to his 400 years' experience of swinging a shafted implement.

In the doctor's pocket he found a letter. Frank? No, he didn't like the sound of Frank, nor the middle initial N. It was signed Bernhard Hassenplug. That was more like it. But Bernhard what? 'Well,' he said out loud in a flat, metallic monotone. 'I am a dropped clanger so I guess that will have to be it: Bernhard C. Langer.

He walked out of the Schloss in search of employment calling for a well-grooved swing. By now his cast-iron frame was completely covered by a layer of skin and human tissue and his head was sprouting a rich harvest of flaxen hair.

18
Creating a Champion

The chairman called the meeting to order. 'I've just come from the Prime Minister's office with a rocket up my arse. For the benefit of new delegates I may say that this commission was set up fifty years ago to present the best side of Australian life to the world. In the beginning we did well. There was hardly a cinema on earth where you were spared a March of Time feature on life saving crews on Bondi beach. Our sportsmen did us proud with blokes like Don, Thommo, Rod Laver, Lew Hoad *and* Evonne Goolagong. We got terrific mileage out of the koala and our film industry won some artistic brownie points among the freakier readers of the *Guardian*.

'Then the rot started, what with Rolf Harris and our cheapo soap operas infiltrating British TV and Sir Les Patterson chundering down his strides on the Royal Command Variety Show. We even lost the Ashes and our international stock went into a nosedive. Now Hawkey demands a new and vigorous initiative to refurbish Australia's image and it's down to us to provide it. This meeting is now open to suggestions and debate.'

The delegate from Queensland rose: 'Traditionally we have got the best value from sportsmen, giving us a reputation as healthy, rugged outdoor people. The downside of this projection has been the fact that so many of our sportsmen have been brainless larrikins interested only in chasing sheilas and cracking tubes. The national profile therefore needs a world-beating sportsman who can string two words together and who can go to a Buckingham Palace garden party without straining the carrots over the geraniums.'

'Thank you, Bruce. Any nominees for this ambassador of the Australian way of life?'

'Some hopes! No, my idea is that this commission draws up a blueprint of the ideal candidate. Then we scour the country for a specimen with the basic raw material and give him the full Svengali treatment. We groom him to our needs. I've had a word with the secret service about our problem. They draw the line at liquidating Paul Hogan, but they are willing to co-operate in brainwashing our man.'

'Brilliant idea,' said the chairman. 'Now let's get down to drawing up the specifications for our archetypical Aussie.'

'Tall and blond,' shouted the delegate from New South Wales.

'Thank you, Bruce.'

'Built like a brick dunny,' offered the delegate from Tasmania.

'Thank you, Bruce.'

'Shoulders as wide as a barn door,' said the Western Australian delegate.

'Thank you, Bruce.'

'Sexy,' proposed the delegate from Victoria.

'Thank you, Sheila.'

'Now what about his brain and character? We know that the mindbenders can work wonders but we must give them something to work with.'

Northern Territory reckoned they might search for years if they pitched their sights too high in the intellectual department.

'Just a basically decent bloke with good hand–eye co-ordination should do the trick.'

'One more detail,' said the chairman. 'We must decide on his sport. Golf is up-market, high profile with plenty of TV exposure, and we seem to have a natural aptitude for the game.'

'We already have a good representation of golf ambassadors,' said Victoria. 'We've got David Graham.'

'David Graham! It defeats me how any Aussie parent could lumber a child with the middle name of Oswald, specially if it made his initials DOG. He's known all over the world as the dog, for Chrissake. Besides he's practically an American; all he can talk about is the Dallas Cowboys.'

Victoria made a desperate attempt to retrieve the situation: 'There's Bruce Crampton.'

Deep silence.

'Can we get back to our vision of the ideal Australian sportsman, or golfer as we seem to have decided? My suggestion is that we circulate the universities, civil-service appointment boards, the armed forces and other government agencies and ask them to contact us immediately if anyone resembling our blueprint presents himself. This commission will reconvene as a selection committee as soon as a likely candidate appears.'

A week later the delegates were back. 'By a stroke of luck we may have found our subject,' said the chairman. 'Our circular arrived just in time to intercept this character as he was about to sign on for fighter pilot training with the RAAF. Lady and gentlemen, I present the face of modern Australia, Mr Peregrine Fauntleroy!'

On walked a tall, young, blond person. 'That name will have to go,' said New South Wales. 'We need something evocative of the rugged outback. Rocky, or Randy, or Craig, or Butch.

'Too Hollywood,' said Victoria. 'How about Greg?' A burst of applause carried the suggestion with acclaim.

'And for the surname I propose resonances of victory, courage and daring on the battlefields, adventurous military enterprises like the Norman Conquest. That's it! Norman. Greg Norman.'

So it was decided, no worries.

'That Nordic look is fine,' said Northern Territory, 'but he is a bit too handsome, almost pretty. He needs a manly, two-fisted appearance to eliminate any suspicion that he might be a wooftah. I know, how about having his nose broken?'

'Good idea,' said the chairman, making a note.

The assessor at the special interrogation unit in the basement of the Defence Ministry building turned the powerful lamp onto the eyes of the apprehensive Norman and prodded him in the chest with his rubber hose.

'Tell me about yourself, sport.'

'Like what?' said Norman.

'Like everything,' said the assessor. 'Like what games do you play. 'Rules', cricket, rugby, surfing, boxing . . . you know, all the games that red-blooded Australian boys play.'

'I'm not really into all that jock stuff. Sometimes I play mah jong with mummy.'

The assessor wrote on the case history: 'Wimp. Aversion therapy. 50,000 volts.'

'What are your interests?'

'I am frightfully fond of natural history.'

The assessor brightened. 'Oh, shooting and fishing eh?'

'Oh no!' said Norman. 'I press wild flowers.'

'Strewth!' The assessor wrote furiously: 'Intensive deprivation treatment. Lobotomy.'

'What about books? Do you read?'

'Rather! I adore the lakeland poets, but my absolute top-yummy favourite is Rupert Brooke. The counterpoint of his tender lyricism and the ultimate futility of war's barbarity is utterly exquisite, don't you agree?'

The assessor groaned. This was no job for the regular shrinks. He wrote: 'Case referred to the Bulgarian. Top priority. All other case work to be reassigned and B must devote himself full time to this one.'

Dr Yankemov, former director of the notorious Kronsky Institut and recent political refugee following the reform of Bulgaria's infamous establishments of political torture, entered Norman's cell with a large hypodermic syringe at the ready.

'This won't hurt a bit,' he murmured with a twisted smile.

They had to put a second layer of felt underlay under the carpet in the offices upstairs to muffle the subterranean screams which continued intermittently for the next three months.

The assessor ushered Norman into the office of the commission chairman.

'He's ready. We've done all we can for him.'

The chairman beamed, noting with satisfaction the improvement wrought by the young man's broken nose. Otherwise there was not a mark on him.

'He plays a pretty good game of golf already,' added the assessor.

'And what do you have to say for yourself, young man?' asked the chairman.

'There's only one point I would like to make, gentlemen,' said Norman, bringing up his knee violently into the assessor's groin.

He leant across the desk and stunned the chairman with a punch in the face, turned and walked out into the sunshine.

'This was no job for the regular shrinks.'

The chairman rose groggily from the floor. The assessor was still bent double, groaning with pain, eyes watering copiously.

'Strewth!' said the chairman. 'We've done it.'

'My oath,' said the assessor. 'He's turned into a real Aussie ripper.'

About the Author

The full member was, as the lawyers say, going about his business when, upon opening the bathroom door, he was confronted by a small bird making furious attacks on the window with its beak. After each frustrated onslaught it pulled out of its spin, opened the throttle and wheeled for another dive.

With the utmost presence of mind the full member went full speed astern, opening every window and door as he retreated and yelping hysterically for help.

At this point a few words may be in order to flesh out the scene. The household is run as far as possible along the lines of a good golf club, with the members occupying the more comfortable quarters and the artisans, or women's section as they sometimes presume to call themselves, in purdah centred on the kitchen.

Even though nearly all the members have long since departed, to pair bond and procreate, they retain country membership including claims to 'their' rooms, free meals and baby-sitting services on demand. So although only the two founder members remain, like wardens of a charity hostel for the indigent, they perforce maintain the conventions of a golf club. The artisan has her domain and the full member has his. The rules are strictly observed; the artisan may, indeed must under the terms of association, tip-toe into the Big Room bearing a cup of coffee every hour on the hour under a vow of silence. Conversation is confined to the neutral territory of the mixed lounge.

The bathroom under discussion adjoins the locker room in the main club and so, in the ordinary way, is out of bounds to the artisans. The emergency meeting of the joint policy committee took place in the mixed lounge.

'There's a bird in the loo!'

'A *bird*? In the *loo*?'

They have quite a lot of conversations of this nature, a perfectly straight-forward statement followed by a probing cross-examination such as might be conducted by a man in a white coat before throwing a net over the patient.

'How could there be a bird in the loo? There's no way for it to get in.'

That was true, as confirmed by the full member during the process of opening doors and windows, all of them previously closed. Equally true was the fact of the bird in the loo. The mystery had all the makings of a prolonged discussion, like the four-hour talkathon when the artisan proposed digging up the asparagus bed, on the flimsy pretext that it yielded no asparagus, and to plant runner beans instead.

It will be remembered that this unhappy episode began with the full member en route to the bathroom. Obviously he had a motive. Equally obviously his objective had not been achieved. This was no time for lengthy debate, or club protocol.

'Come and see.'

The artisan advanced purposefully. The full member was relieved to see the bird, by now in the Big Room and perched on the typewriter. At least he would be spared sarcastic remarks about not having another drink in case he started seeing birds in the loo again. The bird existed and was promptly identified.

'It's a blue tit, female.'

That raised another mystery, requiring further background explanation. In the early days of skirmishing along the matrimonial Maginot Line the full member had adopted the well-tried ploy of psychological warfare of answering the question 'Would you like a piece of cake!' with the booby trap: 'Shop or home-made?'

No effective counter has ever been developed to this weapon. The enemy retires in confusion, either through guilt or fear of the devastating counter-punch: 'No thanks, I'm not very hungry.'

Mind you, the female high command came up with its own version of the verbal landmine. A recent example of this deadly device was used when Hurricane Charlie destroyed the decaying remnants of the bird-box, an inherited pagoda-like structure which was lodged in a fork of the mountain ash.

'You will just have to make a nice replacement. We won't get any songbirds in the garden unless they have somewhere snug and safe for them to nest.'

'Look, if I write one article I shall be finished by lunchtime and it will earn enough for you to buy four bird-boxes at the garden centre.'

'That wouldn't be the same. Still, if you refuse to take the slightest interest in your own home. . . .'

Say so who shouldn't, but when the full member's new bird-box was completed two days later it was everything that a mating pair of songbirds could desire: det., ev. mod. con., adj. grn. blt. For twenty-five years the course has been positively plagued by robins, tits, finches, warblers and thrushes. The day the new nest box was fixed in position they departed in unison, leaving the place to be invaded by squatters in the form of a low-class sparrow. The intruder in the loo was the first up-market bird to be seen on the premises all summer.

Now, no sooner had it been codified by species and gender, than it took off from the typewriter, flew out of the Big Room window, made a wide detour of the new nesting box and departed at high speed in the direction of Sevenoaks.

The artisan withered the full member with the look that says 'I've-got-better-things-to-do-than-waste-my-time-on-your-potty-ideas' and flounced off back to the ghetto. Not before time the full member went to the loo, pondering the mystery of how the blue tit had effected its entry and, more to the point, why.

On returning to his labour the full member tried to pick up his train of thought and focused on the paper in his typewriter. There, unmistakably, was the answer.

It was just another critic.